ANCHOR
BOOKS

TIMES OF TODAY

Edited by

Sarah Marshall

First published in Great Britain in 2004 by
ANCHOR BOOKS
Remus House,
Coltsfoot Drive,
Peterborough, PE2 9JX
Telephone (01733) 898102

All Rights Reserved

Copyright Contributors 2004

SB ISBN 1 84418 333 5

FOREWORD

Anchor Books is a small press, established in 1992, with the aim of promoting readable poetry to as wide an audience as possible.

We hope to establish an outlet for writers of poetry who may have struggled to see their work in print.

The poems presented here have been selected from many entries, and as always editing proved to be a difficult task.

I trust this selection will delight and please the authors and all those who enjoy reading poetry.

Sarah Marshall
Editor

CONTENTS

Which Diagnosis? Or Clarity Begins At Home	Bridget Adams	1
What Do You Do?	Tracey Marie	2
Connection	Joan Prentice	4
For The Sake Of Humanity	O A Oshinbolu	5
Satin Thong	Maureen Westwood O'Hara	6
Absolom Fox 8.5.15 Menin Gate	Roger Newton	8
Let The Train Take The Strain	Mick Nash	9
Aunt Floss, Uncle Dan's Monument	Edmund Saint George Mooney	10
A Cold Day In Hell	David Russell	11
Ramblings	Nikki Rogers	12
Care In The Community	Mai M Roach	13
My Best Guy Friend	Linda Roberts	14
I'm Woman	Jean Shelagh Taylor	15
As By Moonlight	Shane Quinn	16
We've Found Him	Ivor Emlyn Percival	17
The Magic Shire	Julia Pegg	18
Out Of Control 709/17/12/03	Lyn Sandford	19
Ocean	Kathleen Mary Scatchard	20
A Brief Respite	F R Smith	21
That Look	Jo Seward	22
The Old Oak Tree	A C Small	23
Reminisce	Stephanie Stallard	24
Designer Wraps?	Frances Ridett	25
The Sting	R N Taber	26
Comedown	Julie Broadbent	27
Winds Of Change	Carol Olson	28
Summer Beach	Holly Lane	29
Our Little Girl	Jeannette Gaffney	30
Living A Sigh	Carla Iacovetti	31
Sheer Agony	C R Slater	32
Portishead Sunday Night	John Osland	33
Indecision	Clive E Oseman	34
Disillusionment	I Hadenough	35
2012	H G Griffiths	36

Only You	Greta Robinson	37
Life's Gift	C Thornton	38
A Life Of Crime	Richard Trowbridge	39
A Beggar's Life	Lachlan Taylor	40
Andy	Denise Shaw	41
My Garden	Josephine Stimpson	42
Observation Of An Outcast	Smithy	43
The Rose, The Flowers' Queen	Joanna Maria John	44
Medicine With Care	Miriam Jones	45
A W C	M A Woods	46
Goodbye	Julie Wiles	47
I Think	Teresa Whaley	48
Sliming Down 'The Big Red Tomato	Edward James Williams- A Bystander Poet	49
Dialectitis	Brian M Wood	50
Love	Donna Whalley	51
Shilling	Mary Long	52
Love	Josie Lawson	53
Wake Up Sleepyhead	P J Littlefield	54
Thea's Place	Emma M Gascoyne	55
Our Climate	Geoffrey Leech	56
One Day Will I Ever Be Famous	Alison Jane Lambert	57
Mars	D Thomas	58
Black Ducks	Wayne David Knoll	59
The Friday Baking Sun	P J Kemp	60
My Unicorn	Edward Harvey	61
A Yob In Parliament	E L Hannam	62
Gramdad Greenfingers	Kenneth Mood	63
Such A Dear - You Silly Man	Barry Ryan	64
Taken For Granted	June Melbourn	65
Norfolk Tea Room	Joseph McGarraghy	66
Taw Whistles	Amy Alfred Winter	67
'Ships' Of Society	Geoffrey Matthews	68
A Friend Will Always Be There	Tina Rose Dolby	70
A New Year	Diana Daley	71
Sun In The Blue	Carol Ann Darling	72
While You Were Sleeping	Valerie Calvert	74
Another Day Over	George S Johnstone	75

I Felt An Angel's Breath	Ann Hathaway	76
Mixing A Christmas Recipe	Sean Hines	77
Chinese Bowler Man	Suzzette Goddard	78
Humanity	Alan Gordon	79
The True Americans	J F Grainger	80
Season For A King	Joyce Hemsley	81
My Soulmate	Rachael Ford	82
Summer Serenity	Mrinalini Dey	83
I'm Sorry	Norman Andrew Downie	84
The Last Day	Bert Booley	85
Foundations	Patricia Adele Draper	86
Of Royalty	Michael D Bedford	87
Whistling	Peter Mahoney	88
The Path	T Hartley	89
Epistle to D I Brian Tuckwood	John McCartney	90
A Magical Starry Night	Harriet Elizabeth Hobbs	91
To Look Into My Eyes	Maggie Hickinbotham	92
In Search Of Jordan Murdock		
(Aged 14 Years)	Kim Montia	93
The Armed Forces	Brian Lunt	94
Comfort	Linda Pickering	95
Choice - Part 1	Simon Cardy	96
A Name In A Crowd	Eamon John Healy -	
	The Warrior Poet	97
This Land	Dianne Audrey Daniels	98
Untitled	Dale Finlay	99
A Poem For Ariana	Pauline Chiarelli	100
The Voice In My Head	Samantha Walsh	101
Black Silk	Sue Umanski	102
To The Man I've Always Loved	S Longford	103
Be God For The Day	Colin Allsop	104
The Future Now	Renate Fekete	105
Scoop!	John El Wright	106
My Lovely Mum	Hartinajit Kaur Dulay	107
Anarchy In The UK	Chris T Barber	108
The Last Will And		
Testament Of Rex King	Christopher Higgins	109
African Blush	Jan Ross	110

Many More . . .	Jodi Wheeler	111
Mother's Day	Karandip Kaur Dulay	112
Untitled	P Allen	113
Dandelion Sculpture	Allan Pow	114
Pie In The Sky	Sid De Knees	115
Never Deceiving And Never Deceived	Jesu Ah'so	116
Were I To Meet A Wizard	Mary Frances Mooney	117
Postcards	Tracey Marie	118
Sorely Missed	Jeff Brooks	119
Don't Underestimate The Colour Red	Ian Bowen	120
I Stand Alone	L Baynes	121
The Proposal Of Marriage	Steven Borysewicz	122
Loss Leaders	John Belcher	123
A Dance Of Time	Marj Busby	124
The Buffalo	David A Bray	125
Axe The TV Licence Fee!	D K F Martindale	126
Stream	R Mills	127
Untitled	Edward Hill	128
The Taurus Man	Ellen Chambers	129
Undergraduates Underground	John Delaney	130
September Eleven	E F Croker	131
Journey's End	M J Chadwick	132
Clever	Jackie Jones-Cahill	133
The Lines Of Life	Jay Berkowitz	134
Fully Booked Insania	Vann Scytere	135
You . . . Complete Me	Irene Reid	136
My Great Mummy	Jovan Dulay	137
Midnight Lover	Myra Selvadurai	138
Noises In The Night	Wendy Wordsworth	139
Ireland's Immigrant	B M F	140
Dark	Catrina Lawrence	141
Little Angel	Atlanta Oakes	142
Editors	John J Flint	143
Just Be Glad	Margaret Upson	144
1915	Gatekeeper	145
Music On Menace	Paul Volante	146

Just Imagine	Zahraa Mughal	147
The Love Inside	Colin Morrow	148
Phantom Crossword Solver	Philip McLynn	149
April Snow	R Martin	150
I Saw Your Letter Of Denial	Graham Hare	151
Separation	Robert McIlveen	152
Worry	Nicola Joy Moore	153
Letter To The Better	Nacala Makiin	154

WHICH DIAGNOSIS? OR CLARITY BEGINS AT HOME

If my house strikes you as dirty
Pity me
For I am lonely and depressed
And don't know what to do

If my house strikes you as clean
Pity me
For I am lonely and depressed
And don't know what else to do

If my house strikes you as dirty
Envy me
For I am happy and fulfilled
And have other things to do

If my house strikes you as clean
Envy me
For I am happy and fulfilled
And have someone in to 'do'.

If my house strikes you as dirty
Rouse me
For I am dull and slow
And can't get into a routine

If my house strikes you as clean
Rouse me
For I am dull and slow
And can't get out of my routine

If my house strikes you as dirty
Soothe me
For I am tense and agitated
Running round in useless circles

If my house strikes you as clean
Soothe me
For I am tense and agitated
Running round in needless circles

If my home feels friendly,
Come on in

Bridget Adams

WHAT DO YOU DO?

What do you value?
The air that you breathe
What do you value?
Nothing until you grieve

The loss after all is gone
No need to look at the sun
The moon and the stars in the sky
The value of what's passed you by

Why can't we value
While we have the chance?
Why can't we value
That passing glance

Of life and all its beauty?
When we can see all we want to see
To hear the ocean, feel the breeze
To see the autumn falling leaves
To feel fresh snowflakes on your face
Little children dressed in ribbons and lace

We stop yet we don't value
What we have before us
We stop and we don't value
It's just ignored by us.

Until the day that they're all gone
No longer to stand and look at the sun
Feel the wind upon our face
See our children all dressed in lace

Awake to a beautiful blue sky
And stop and value and wonder why
We take for granted all these pleasures
Mother Nature filled with such measures
Of what we stop and feel no need to value
They're only put there for me and you
So please take time to consider
What life has to show you
And next time you see them
Understand their value.

Tracey Marie

CONNECTION

Mars, the red planet billion miles from us
Is sending out signals, sounds like a buzz
Do they have bodies? Or just look like bugs
Slant eyes, no noses and very big lugs?

What happens if they get a very bad cold?
Where does their snot go? Out of their toes!
And what about phlegm? Does it lie in their chest
Or, come out like piddle? Bet that makes a mess!

Of course I'm supposing but don't really know
Might they communicate on their mobile phones?
Perhaps we should ignore their signals to Earth
They might want asylum, and that would be worse.

We have quite a mixture on Earth as it is
We want to keep noses, not ears that whizz!
More patients for hospital, who can't get a bed
Let's all go to Mars, and live there instead.

Joan Prentice

FOR THE SAKE OF HUMANITY

God bless all who are helping humanity,
Peace and love to you all,
Thank you for your bravery and service
The world is a better place because of you.
My grandfather says,
When the going gets tough
Do not take the easy route.
May you never walk alone,
But always surrounded in God's love, healing and angel rays,
Sending you a rainbow of roses.
xxxxx with love xxxxx

O A Oshinbolu

SATIN THONG

Listening to the sounds of laughter
About the times last night, and after
Waking up and wondering what went on
Did you misplace your satin thong?

It seemed okay to much imbibe
And think of how you could contrive
To make him look upon your frock
Inhibitions here, could take a knock!

It worked alright as booze ran down
And made you smile instead of frown
The night was fine, and you he picked
In a frenzy as your tonsils he licked!

But I should really settle on down
Or else I'll peak too soon, then frown
If I did not receive that first hot kiss
Preliminary, of course, to that night's bliss!

Well clubbing finished 'Yours or mine?'
Those were the usual words, I find
I went to his, and drank some more
And sorted out, that final score.

He lost his will, but still I tried
That passion riding high inside
But booze had won, and he, under zest
Looked to me to have lost his interest!

So I tried again to re-deliver
But he thought only of his liver
He snored and chanted, 'Let's get undressed'
Not knowing I had tried, and now distressed

To think I'd worked hard to sing his song
And ended up, missing my satin thong

So be beware of love's fine song
Of wearing your beloved satin thong
Make sure you get a man, well tested
Before your thong is reinvested!

Maureen Westwood O'Hara

ABSALOM FOX 8.5.15 MENIN GATE

Who knows where Absalom has gone
To Earth? His valiant soul set free,
From further pain; his duty done;
Accompanied by the lost crowd,
Unlike the fox, but son of man
With no known place to lay their head.

And when the news broke, he was dead,
As down his face the hot tears ran,
Did his stunned father cry aloud,
'O, Absalom, my son, my son,
Would, God, that I had died for thee:
O, Absalom, my son, my son?'

Roger Newton

LET THE TRAIN TAKE THE STRAIN

An Indian brave called 'Numbut'
Had to travel to join his tribe,
As the journey would have took weeks by foot,
The iron horse of the paleface he'd ride:
He didn't have very much wampum,
So the train man said, 'We'll take you there,
We don't want your money, young Redskin,
Because Numbut the brave deserves the fare!'

Mick Nash

AUNT FLOSS, UNCLE DAN'S MONUMENT
(Dedicated with love to Aunt Floss, Uncle Dan)

Stone locked in stone smooth to flatter
Her death amongst angry branches:

Instant curves cutting volume
Through winter's old landscapes:

Image clamped against the sun,
Riveting soul, silver, shade, to
Feet curved around into monument,
Not a head even, winter stone:

A bolt of wood pushed, round, down,
Into symmetry: shoulders flexed in wire,

A clavicle, caged, brawn, knotted in iron strands,
Perspective in unison, power, bunched, form.

Edmund Saint George Mooney

A COLD DAY IN HELL

I was never afraid to die, but I never thought much about it before,
I mean, not how things would be if I couldn't wake up anymore.
I was too busy for God, and He seemed too busy for me,
I said, 'A believer is something I can't be,
This faith business is for someone else.'
Now I know He didn't die for Himself.
I didn't have time for anything I couldn't see.
Funny, I didn't see this place, now it's all around me.
I've seen a lot here I know, all dead.
I wanted to tell Mum I love her, but there's nothing to be said.
John Lennon's over there, but no one will let him bow.
He's still singing 'Imagine there's no Heaven,' but sounds
                                    different now.
I've got a toothache that doesn't end. No dentists here.
Got an upset stomach too, from twenty years of beer.
'It'll be a cold day in Hell when I believe in God,' I said;
Strange, every day's cold down here when you're dead.
I lived a good life, God but I never listened to You,
I guess I'm paying for it now, but when's my sentence through?
Please God, my wife and kids, I just want to say goodbye,
And tell them just to trust You, for some day soon they'll die.

David Russell

RAMBLINGS

Getting there gradually
But not there yet
That place I need to be
A place that gets me back to me

Thoughts and emotions
Running through my head
What ifs and would bes
Why did you have to leave?

Tears of laughter and tears of pain
They never go away
And sometimes I need to fight
So late into the night

Thoughts, emotions, laughter and pain
All because of you
And I know one day I'll be fine
But how I wish you were never mine.

Nikki Rogers

CARE IN THE COMMUNITY

'Good morning, I'm your new home help - now tell me what to do
You know we don't clean windows, or scrub around the loo.

I'll get the coal in first, I think, then rake a bit at fire
You'd best get up while I do this - get into day attire.

What's that? - You're cold with open doors - the fire's gone so low
I'll put some coal on now my dear - there is a tiny glow.

What now? - You need a hand to rise - but look, my hands are black
Where is your bathroom? - To the right? - Lie there, I'll be right back.

I'll put the kettle on to boil and make a cup of tea
Now grab my arm, I'll pull you up - just take a grip of me.

What did you say? - Your hands are stiff, and very painful too -
Then stay in bed today, my dear, and tell me what to do.

Look at the time - my, how it flies - as yet I have done nowt
Oh look! - I've smothered up the fire - the blooming thing's gone out.

I'll have to leave you now my dear - the time has simply flown
Half an hour's all they gave - so now you're on your own.

Mai M Roach

MY BEST GUY FRIEND

My friend is a real cool guy named Gary
He always makes me laugh, and so happy,
And he's very thoughtful, generous and kind
The best guy friend that I could ever find.

Every week lots of letters to me he does send
Jobs he does, my garden seat he did mend,
Love to hear his fab voice on the phone
When he calls me from his mobile or home.

Not living near, I don't see him very much
By writing and phoning we keep in touch,
When we do meet, I love whatever we do
Like feeding the ducks and seagulls; he does too.

When I am with him, do enjoy his company
Time just seems to whizz by, when with Gary,
We chat away for hours and get on so well
He calls me Kid Lindy, feel like a little girl.

We can tease each other with things we say
Neither of us gets upset, so it's really okay,
Seem to be always making each other laugh
Even if it's over something we said that was daft.

Flying kites, writing names in the sand, such fun
Makes us feel like kids again - still so young,
Buying me so much, I thank him for everything
My best guy friend, Gary Russell Farthing.

Linda Roberts

I'm Woman

I'm the whisper of a summer breeze,
I'm winter's chill to make you freeze,
I'm the softest touch of a kitten's paw,
I'm the lion, when crossed, I roar,
I'm the sun and the moon,
I'm the darkness of a tomb,
I'm the weakest little mouse,
I'm the ox as strong as a house,
I'm the rain to make things grow,
I'm the coldest winter's snow,
I'm the cooling hand on a fevered head,
I'm the one who says what needs to be said,
I'm the lover, the friend, the wife,
I'm the one true love of your life,
      I'm woman!

Jean Shelagh Taylor

AS BY MOONLIGHT

As by moonlight couples kiss,
And they miss,
The day of theirs,
But now all they do is stare,
And I wonder if they see,
All that is me?

Shane Quinn

WE'VE FOUND HIM!

The soldiers searched for seven long months,
But Saddam could not be found,
But as a result of a tip-off, they heard,
He had gone underground.
He had lived in marble palaces, he had a yacht anchored in the bay,
He had weapons of mass destruction, in mass graves,
                                    thousands of his people lay,
Tortured and maimed by his regime, and murdered day by day.

600 soldiers were drafted, all of them armed to the teeth,
To search and find Saddam Hussein, was the object of their brief,
They approached a house in the country, the interior was untidy
                                    and grim,
They arrested two men with rifles, who lay waiting within,
Under a rug, in an outbuilding, they uncovered a hole,
An unkempt scruffy person appeared, he looked like he had
                                    been digging coal.

'I am the President of Iraq, I wish to negotiate with you.'
An American soldier with a rye grin said,
'President Bush sends his regards too!'

He was taken into custody, the world rejoiced. He will stand trial.

Ivor Emlyn Percival

This Magic Shire

I claim this to be a magic shire.
Staffordshire, on its northern border,
The centuries-old home of 'the potters'.
Coal lay beneath the cold, red clay here.
Did not God form man from such earth?
These clever artisans, transforming the red clay,
With the help of cleansing fire,
Turning clay into terracotta stone,
Aided by the local spring waters,
And the skilled turner's hands.
Slowly drying before firing,
Aided by the chill, moorland air.
How the four elements came together.
The diversely skilled pottery workers,
Seemed to hold the power of magic,
In the true craftsman's passion.
This skill several aeons old.
For it was ancient before the rise,
Of glorious Egypt, Greece and Rome.
Its skill held on an equal par,
To the guild of the metalworkers,
Who in the bronze age,
Drew Arthur's sword from the stone.
The beaker people and the Celts,
Called this bleak place their home.
Here Romans made pots for their legends,
In the vale of Trent, two thousand years ago.
Much benign magic is bound in the local clay,
Transformed over passing centuries, so today.

Julia Pegg

OUT OF CONTROL 709/17/12/03

A body
Has been violated.
The heart's no longer
At peace.
A spirit of quiet
And restfulness
Is now open to the winds.

What had been
Contentment
Is now fear
And pain.
Warmth of love
And compassion -
Shattered once again.

As downward
Goes the spiral
And night breaks into day,
Hurt and bitter anger -
Unlike hope -
May fade away.

Lyn Sandford

OCEAN

The sea is a creature,
Sometimes placid, calm,
Ebbing and flowing,
Knowing the moon's moods,
Rulings.

Then changing from passive,
To activity,
Rolling and foaming,
Like sudden hillsides rising.

Wet, yet seeming solid,
A powerful force,
That works upon the
Imagination,
Strangely.

Where cold, dark chasms yawn,
As waves bend and curl,
Into huge curved claws,
That snatch and rage at,
The shore.

Destructive without hate,
Creative without love,
Having no conscience,
Or will, innocent,
Timeless.

Kathleen Mary Scatchard

A BRIEF RESPITE

I am feeble now and weary, my laboured breath comes fast
As I stumble on towards the end of my lonely road at last,
I pause to look back at the road that has led me there,
And see a pathway strewn with pitfalls, sorrow, grief and care.

At first it was a happy road, a smooth and tranquil way,
Bathed in sunshine, joy and laughter - life was a carefree holiday,
For companions, I had kinsfolk, whose kind and loving care
Guided my footsteps surely, past every fretting snag and snare.

Suddenly, with a last farewell from tired and toil-worn hands,
They were gone, and I was alone on Life's bare shifting sands,
Sorrowing and uncertain, and bereft of an earthly friend
On the road I had to follow, there seemed to be no end.

I moved slowly onwards, through heartache, toil and pain,
Sometimes I walked in sunshine, but more often it was in rain,
Reeling and stumbling wildly at each adversity until
I now stand alone and exhausted at the top of my lonely hill.

Here I will rest awhile to savour life's last fleeting lease,
Uncertain as to how long 'twill be ere my brief lifespan will cease,
To reflect upon the many blessings I have enjoyed along the way,
Before I'm laid to rest at last 'neath earth's green overlay.

What destiny lies ahead of me? I gaze with anxious eyes,
I can see no guiding beacon light beneath the lowering skies,
A veil hangs over the valley where my steps still have to tread,
But I must follow with unflagging faith where my ancestors have led.

I am rested now and reassured - I can resume my earthly stride,
No longer do I walk alone, there are others at my side,
The outstretched arms of those I love are reaching out to me
Pointing the way to paradise and the promise of eternity!

F R Smith

THAT LOOK

I can't forget your face
    It was time to say goodbye
That look will stay with me always
    Oh how it made me cry

We could not stay together
    Our lives we must spend apart
Waving farewell to you
    Has surely broken my heart

I cannot think of a future
    Without you by my side
I hope and pray that one day
    Our paths will again collide.

Jo Seward

THE OLD OAK TREE

Precious child whose years number three
Inquisitive eyes gazing up at me,
I am the old oak tree
I shall watch over thee.

On your return bring your friends
When humid days have no end,
Let your angelic voices sing
Happily dance, climb and swing,
I am the old oak tree
I shall give support to thee.

Come and hide from September rain
With your first love, carve her name,
Make promises sealed with kisses
Share your hopes, dreams and wishes,
I am the old oak tree
I shall give shelter to thee.

So cut me down, chop me up
Make paper planes and firewood,
But I am the old oak tree
Forever rooted in your memory.

A C Small

REMINISCE

Isn't it funny when you reminisce,
Things once talked about, and things you missed,
Laughing and joking, special moments shared,
Faces and people that you know cared.

I once came across that certain face,
Shame about the timing and the wrong place,
But things always change as time goes by,
And who am I to reason why?

Everyone knows that time doesn't stand still,
And most things come if you have a strong will,
As long as you want and need bad enough,
Life really doesn't have to turn out so tough.

Opportunities happen - and come what may,
You should grasp at your chances and hope that they stay,
Every hope, every dream, every meaningful kiss,
Should be kept well alive - not be left to reminisce . . .

Stephanie Stallard

DESIGNER WRAPS?

The cold on the ground and the fear that surrounds,
A blanket? A box? Odd shoes and no socks?
But think I to myself, as I glance, quickly pass,
A home you must have, somewhere in the past.
This surely must be the greatest defeat,
When you find your home is on the street,
But not in house or flat up high,
But on the pavement, under night's sky.
In the doorway you sleep of a shop, oh so dear,
Such luxuries so far from you as you lie so near.
If you're lucky tonight you may find that your wrap,
Is a Hillfiger or Gucci, in which you nap.
But not for the clothes to have, do you strive,
But the box so strong in which they arrive.

Frances Ridett

THE STING

Hit a bee with a magazine,
it responded by chasing me
across the village green;
I ran into a church, slammed
the door shut - but the bee
found a crack, poised to attack
as I cowered in a pew,
wondering what on earth to do!
For wasn't this God's house,
the bee, one of His creatures,
and wasn't I the aggressor, no
real provocation, only suspicion
it might mean me harm
so what did I think I was doing
when I raised my arm
instinctively, without thinking?
A natural reaction, I hear
you agree. So, too, that sting
taunting, haunting me still
with the merry buzzing of a bee
I never meant to kill

R N Taber

COMEDOWN

I'm riding high on the skyline,
But I'm balancing on the edge.
See, look up and touch the sky,
See, look up and make a wish tonight.
I'm riding high on the skyline.
Can you see down below?
I'm beyond my depth of what isn't known.
I'm coming down so fast,
So fast in fact I think I might hit the ground.
I'm riding high above the horizon,
But I'm no longer balancing on the edge.
I've looked up and touched the sky,
I've looked up and made a wish tonight.
I'm riding high above the horizon.
Can you see down below?
I'm within the depth of what isn't known.
I'm still falling fast.
So fast that I can almost touch the ground.
You're down below,
And you're beyond the depth of what isn't known.
Can you see me falling?
Falling down so fast onto the ground.
Caught within the comedown,
Caught so bad we've tried to leave.

Julie Broadbent

WINDS OF CHANGE

Winds of change blow on today . . .
Throughout the years of history . . .
Do you hear the winds of change
Blowing over prairies, and the mountain range?
Inviting winds blow on and on . . .
Just as the tides roll in and are gone . . .
The winds of change bring in ideas fresh and new . . .
Invigorating thoughts that challenge you . . .

Carol Olson

SUMMER BEACH

It's nice on the beach in the hot sun,
Having a paddle, having fun.

Take your bucket and spade,
Bring a big umbrella for shade.
Put on lots of sun cream
To protect you from the sun.

My sandcastle is crumbling,
Digging a hole, don't fall in.
Children playing in sand dunes and hiding in caves,
And I can see lots of people in the waves.

Put your ice cream rubbish in the bin.
It must be lunchtime, my tummy's rumbling.

It's nice on the beach in the hot sun,
Having a paddle, having fun.

Holly Lane

OUR LITTLE GIRL

You have grown so independent
Getting taller with each day
You can hold a conversation
In the cutest kind of way
You are my ray of sunshine
Fill the house with so much love
At three you dress yourself
And know what colour goes with what
I love your cuddles daily
Tell me what you'd like to eat
When the phone rings rush to answer
'Cause you're the first to speak
When it's bedtime, like an angel
You will sleep until the morn
Thank Heaven we were really blessed
The day that you were born.

Jeanette Gaffney

LIVING A SIGH

'This mountain seems high
and hard to climb,'
she said, lying upon her bed.
Living in the wait
is more difficult
than looking for a
horizon
with blind eyes.
Life is sometimes complex
and yet . . .

I should really cast off
the desire of longing,
ridding myself
of the repugnant notion
that possibility
is just around the corner,
lurking,
waiting to fall upon me
like hail descending
from a bursting sky.
Pondering such thoughts
only intensifies this manifested
prurience
and at present
I am left to a simple
sigh.

Carla Iacovetti

SHEER AGONY

I put my hands together, with no idea what for.
I only knew that I could not face life, not anymore.
I sat in desperation, a streetlight was all aglow,
Silent tears crying in my heart, only few so know.
My hands were clasping tightly, no will left at all,
I felt as if a waste of space, extremely ever so small.
Eyes did not shed a single tear; none were left to cry,
Painful agony so many emotions were running dry.
One word alone with clenched teeth, strength let utter
Yet even that word ached my heart with a mutter,
I had no strength at all within me, left then to sigh,
Just this word of thought speaking multitudes, why?
My reasoning for this real and sorry sad old state,
I fear is painful for me to divulge, or deliberate.
Yet my very emotion, my thought, you may well find,
Will one day, surely, echo within your very own mind.
For life alone, with all its crazy madness and play,
Will bring such great grief, and emotion your way.
It may be through one of many, endless, simple things,
So be ever prepared for the pain, life often brings.

C R Slater

PORTISHEAD SUNDAY NIGHT
(For Sue)

Flickering lights on that distant shoreline
Like your eyes watching over my fears
While an infinity of stars glimmer above
To the calm ocean's voice, in my ears.

'I'm there for you,' those whispers say
As they gently lap, here at my shore
And the light from your eyes will show me the way
How could anyone ask you for more?

Later, restless in sleep, I hear your soft voice
But turning, I find you're not there
Though now I have warm memories of you,
Your lips touch; and the smell of your hair.

This morning we spoke, the memory was there
I just know it will always be here
It'll warm me now, whenever I'm down
And even more, when I know that you're near.

John Osland

INDECISION

My brain is crippled with indecision.
No one wants a soul trapped in a prison,
but the escape route is fraught with sorrow.
If I leave it gives my heart time to heal
with a promise of a bright tomorrow.
But will I find tranquillity and steal
some sunshine to thaw the frozen wastelands
of a life too often cruelly sullied?
Or will the shadow of guilt follow me
wherever my tortured mind has scurried,
never allowing me the right to see
how wonderful this short life ought to be?

Clive E Oseman

DISILLUSIONMENT

Are you guiding a child in a choice of career?
If reading is 'hearing', then give me your ear.
To every young person, I'd say 'Do not make
The same choice as I did, for it was a mistake.'
There are people like me in all parts of the land,
And supply far exceeds the employers' demand.
This further reduces the salaries paid
From the dwindling profits the business has made.
Any increases are said to depend
On the money brought in by the bills which you send,
But often a bill, which was based on their charge
For my time, was reduced as they thought it too large.
'Cut-throat' competition has whittled away
The charges which clients are requested to pay.
This means, of course, that profit margins decrease,
And the volume of work therefore needs to *in*crease.
Thus the fee earners assuredly will
Feel obliged to work longer, just to 'stand still'.
My starting point may be quite common, I fear,
For a qualified man: 7,000 a year.
The typists got 'peanuts', which I understood;
Though friendly and willing, they weren't very good.
Policing their errors took hours of each day;
Precious fee-earning time draining away.
I obtained a new job with a promising firm,
But my boss's demands took an unwelcome turn.
Unattainable financial targets were set,
Which made my accepting the job a regret.
I resigned before long, and shall practise no more.
For goodness' sake, don't be a solicitor.

I Hadenough

2012

London hosting the Olympics
Of the 30th Olympiad
The UK winning nearly all gold medals
The best sport we have ever had

Queen's Diamond Jubilee year
Celebrations all the better
Because of London's 'Games' going on
Everyone cheering to the letter.

First Earth City on the Earth Moon
Launching manned mission to Mars
Then perhaps to who knows where?
Among the other stars?

H G Griffiths

ONLY YOU

Love led me to a place
where there was only your face
I stumbled in, my heart aflame
heard you call my name.
Now I reach for you
but you're not there
and still you keep saying
you really care.
Now I'm turning round
running from the sound
of your heart next to mine
searching for a sign
that these tears will end
like April rain.
Hoping for a way I might love again
but we both know it's true
there can only be you.

Greta Robinson

LIFE'S GIFT

Time is precious, live it full,
experience shares, a fruitful pull
you out of blankest greyest day,
tedious nonsense, wastes away,
your lifelong age, in stupid cant,
what's the worth, of expedient,
telling you, do this do that,
empty meaning, hollow phrase,
foolish natter, tries to praise,
the strong from doing, what is best,
for living, sharing, that's the test,
your desire, to do what's right,
sense in reason, lives to spite,
traitors here and cowards there,
shameful face is hiding; where?
Know not we, that we should care,
let them stand, or do they dare?
Crawl back whence, to loathsome lair,
where nothing's done, for them no share,
in our delight at battles where,
wars are won, to prove we care,
for beautiful girl of shimmering hair,
loves in wonder, a life to spare.

C Thornton

A LIFE OF CRIME

I thought it was time
To start on a life of crime
Shoplifting
Well with my family background it seemed fitting
So I went to a department store
One I've been to many times before
And took scarf and stuffed it down my knicker
The store detective grabbed me, I should have been quicker
She took me to the office and said, 'Take your knickers down'
I thought she would let me off if I gave her a nasty frown
But she called the 'law'
They came and dragged me out the door
Then I was up before the beak
He wouldn't give me a chance to speak
So I gave him a nasty frown
I'm sure his wig nearly fell down
And with a nervous cough
He said, 'I'm going to let you off
But don't you let me see you here again.'
Don't laugh, I've just been nicked in Spain!

Richard Trowbridge

A Beggar's Life

A beggar stopped me in the street
    asking for money to buy a meal
It made me wonder about this life
    as to me it is so unreal.

Why should humans have to beg?
    Is it because they've lost their pride
When they cannot find a job
    and it's on begging which they decide

We have situations with the beggars
    where people shun those without a job
But most of those that do are opulent
    who project themselves as snobs.

There are many reasons we have beggars
    most are from marriages breaking down
Where the husband turns to alcohol
    and joins the Skid Row in the town.

There are beggars shy and reticent
    who haven't much conversation
And because they have lived a life alone
    they join in with this alienation.

Lachlan Taylor

ANDY

My nurse Andy you must meet,
His skills and talents are hard to beat.
He's good, he's caring and he's kind
He understands my heart and mind.

He's the only man I really trust
This man with hair that's of the reddish rust.
He has freckles that go up his arms
He's full of life and full of charm.

His gentle patience makes me safe
For I am but a mental straying waif.
He put me together from a broken pot
This nurse of mine, he's got the lot.

He taught me how to start to read
He's perfect in his every deed.
I swear to God, he was sent to me
He's unlocked my mind with a golden key.

This love I feel is good and great
From his ideas I do create.
I cried to God when I was lame
A wild thing then but now I'm tame.

Denise Shaw

MY GARDEN

In my garden I would like to see
An array of colours looking at me
Roses, pansies, that kind of thing
Not bugs and slugs and nettles that sting
Maybe some fish in a little pond
Oh, Fairy Godmother, I need your wand!

I've bought some tools and things to sow
On with my wellies and off I go
Watch out, bugs, you'd better hide
The roses and pansies are on my side

A few weeks later, I can see
A patch of ground that is weed-free
I've sown my flowers and veggies too
But listen, bugs, I'm not through with you

There's a compost heap behind the shed
Now off with you, there's your bed
Take your friends along with you
Vacate my garden, go on, shoo!

Josephine Stimpson

OBSERVATIONS OF AN OUTCAST

Twilight in the city, afternoon drawing to a close,
Standing on a street corner all alone.
Nothing to do, I'm on my own,
No place to go, nothing waiting at home.
Black eyes, white face, chains and studs
3-inch spikes on steel-capped boots.
Look so different, feel the same,
Watching all the people walking down the lane.

People who scrutinise you but never see your face,
People who don't see past their own little space,
People who see you and forget a moment later,
People who store you away in their memory forever.
People who'll describe your face whenever there's a crime,
People who don't really care so long as they're on time,
Children who look up at you with innocent's gaze,
Anxious mothers who take one look and pull their kids away.
Young men with eager faces and their fortunes to earn,
Older men who're confident they have nothing more to learn,
People who walk past you with their noses in the air,
Busy sort of people don't even notice that you're there.
Happy-looking fellows with families at home,
People wearing signs advertising a shop, a car, a phone,
People who avoid you, unconsciously it seems,
People who will pointedly cross over to another street.
Self-righteous people loudly discussing riff-raff and their crimes,
People who will look away, never meet your eyes,
Women who declare you make them feel quite weak,
Gossips who are sure they saw you at a mugging, just last week,

Not one of all these people goes beyond what they can see,
And no one bothers to find out whether it is the real me.
When you're a city kid, and you're on the 'trouble' list,
To the general populace, you don't even exist.

Smithy

THE ROSE, THE FLOWERS' QUEEN

I have a long green sturdy stem with green leaves and prickly thorns,
I grow in an earthen bed near freshly mowed lawns,
I love to wake up to all the warm sunny morns,
I close my petals just before twilight,
I look forward to each warm silent night,
My buds are sticky like glue,
One bloom appears, then two, just like a twin,
Bees love to collect my sweet nectar deep within,
Another bloom appears then there are three,
We love to keep each other company,
We grow close together, cheek to cheek,
By midsummer we're at our peak,
I love the humidity and the tranquillity,
I'm the flowers' queen,
I love the showers that fall that make me feel so fresh and clean,
I love to hear everyone's praises,
Summer truly amazes,
My cheeks are rosy,
I'm made into a posy,
I love each day that's so warm and cosy,
Or I'm made into a bouquet,
I love to dance in summer's cabaret
While summer's clock is ticking away,
When summer is in decline,
No more am I the colour of sparkling red wine.

Joanna Maria John

MEDICINE WITH CARE

Locked in a cupboard, or a shelf up high
Away from little eyes that spy
That's the place to keep your pills
Medicines and cures for all your ills

But beware!
Don't take the wrong one
Cos in a flash you might be gone
Off to the hospital you will go
With a 'Ooh-ah-ooh'
And a 'No! No! No!'

So listen to your doctor's advice
Read the label once or twice
Then you won't ever take the wrong pill
And you won't have to leave your will.

Miriam Jones

A W C

Patient and kind and understanding,
Many stairs with lots of landings,
Room to climb, and room to rest,
Mother Centre, you are the best!

You take us to your bosom with a warm embrace,
Thank you for providing this nourishing place.
A place where we are all accepted for who we are,
A secret combination to help us go far.

Gentle and supportive and willing and wise,
Selflessly giving without any ties.
Thank you for being our Community Mother
And showing your love like no other.

M A Woods

GOODBYE

Yes, now is the time
We must say goodbye
All because of a white lie
Now I know you did love me.

Julie Wiles

I THINK

I think
but I don't know why
I dream
and in my sleep I cry
I wonder
every day is the same
I hope
but hope is insane
and then
there is a void
a place
of nothingness inside
strange
how we cannot hide
I think
but I don't know why
I dream
to dream is to die
to lose
and there be nothing to regain
to be crazy
lest we be sane.

Teresa Whaley

SLIMMING DOWN 'THE BIG RED TOMATO'
(This poem is just for you, Jimmy)

Fat Jimmy Whitaker, our Saturday hack.
      Is down on the carpet, flat on his back;
Threshing around like a big white whale,
      All that's missing is a triangular tail.

Running around with a sagging belly,
      He's looking like a strawberry jelly;
Trying his best to lose three stones,
      He'd rather look like a bag of bones.

Once young and fit, and looking svelte,
      He now has a job to do up his belt;
He must exercise greatly to reduce that tum,
      Although he'll find it's really no fun.

Those fattening foods he must forego,
      If high weight-loss he intends to show;
As one of a team he must try his best,
      Until he looks good when just in a vest.

But always for Jimmy the greatest pain,
      Will be resisting a glass of champagne;
For like himself it's fizzy and bubbly,
      And has him murmuring, 'Lovely jubbly.'

We all will watch him follow his plan,
      To see if it reveals the 'inner man';
For with all his efforts his body to slim,
      He better be careful, and not get too thin!

The lesson for us all to learn,
      Is when the fat you have to burn,
To exercise may do you good,
      But don't do more than you really should.

Edward James Williams - A Bystander Poet

DIALECTITIS

I've just got your message,
Which I can't understand -
The language must come
From a far distant land.

I've spoken with people
From all round the world -
But the words you have sent
Are the strangest I've heard.

I'm fluent in 'Yorkshire',
Welsh and Gaelic I speak -
Yet, speech from the 'Midlands'
To me, it's all 'Greek'.

I know it sounds silly
That I seem so dumb -
But, you'll have to translate
The weird language of 'Brum'!

Brian M Wood

LOVE

Love is a firework waiting to explode
Love is a double barrel - ready to load
Love is sharing ice cream with only one spoon
Love is sleeping side by side under the stars and moon
Love is agile and love is hard and strong
Love is black lacy bras and a minuscule thong
Love is a flickering candle - burning deep and slow
Love is feeling on top of the world and strangely low
Love is safe and comforting in enveloping arms
Love is a Mediterranean ocean so peaceful and calm
Love is the reason why and a cover for every mistake
Love is there to greet you each morning when you awake
Love is a soppy movie on a cold winter's night
Love is the passionate make-up kiss after a fight
Love is a fairy-tale story of me and you
Love is incomparable and love takes two.

Donna Whalley

SHILLING

I saw it shining on the ground
It was a shilling I had found.
I gazed upon my lucky find
To spend and quickly in my mind.
Then I thought of those in need
And felt ashamed of my greed.
I was not in need of a slice of bread
So I read again what my bible said.
I looked at the shilling in my hand
Many poor people filled our land.
The shilling must go to those in need
And shame upon me for my greed.
The workhouse just down the street
With this shilling some would eat.
So I knocked upon the big oak door
Then said 'I'm sorry it is not more.
I found it there upon the ground,
So I give to you what I have found.'
A tear rolled down the lady's cheek
She took the shilling for food to seek.
That night again my bible I read
I knew that lady was now well fed.
I did not need that shilling you see
Gran said that our Lord had tested me.

Mary Long

LOVE

Nearly thirteen years ago
My daughter gave birth to my first grandchild
Now, nearly thirteen years later
My first grandchild emails me
Her name is Michelle.
I love my granddaughter
I love my other granddaughter
Her name is Katie
I love my first grandson
His name is Callum
And I love my last grandson
His name is Alfie
I feel so blessed having four grandchildren
When I first used a computer
It was at Sussex University in conjunction with
'New Horizons' back in 1979
This was a sponsored course in conjunction with
The Friends Centre, of Brighton
So much happens as the years go by
So much . . . isn't it lovely?
Email from grandchildren . . .
It is now nearly Christmas 2003
God bless darlings and don't forget
Give Mummy a kiss from me.
I love her too . . .

Nanny Josie

Josie Lawson

WAKE UP SLEEPYHEAD

Once in the land of nod,
Children's dreams often seem so real, so true,
You are Spiderman or Superman,
Batman and Robin are your pals,
Adventures in sleep are set for you,

You save the princess from the dragon,
Place her back on the throne,
Then hold up the bridge single-handedly,
While urgent repairs are made,
Then swim with the crocodiles before you get home.

The bank robbers dropped their guns and ran,
When they saw you arrive,
Hiding away in the metropolis,
Thanking their lucky stars,
That they were still alive.

Later you skied down Mount Everest,
Then jumped the Eiffel Tower,
We were all astounded by your strength and ability,
Not to mention your dash and power,

Then you helped an old man in the street who had lost his glasses,
Taking him to an optician for the best pair money could buy,
Then to the moon on your new kite,
Your best friends, Alex and Joe,
With you tried to fly.

When you wake in the morning,
Full of where and what you've done,
Picking up your school bus from the corner,
Carrying your school bag full of books,
But you pretend it contains a secret map and the latest immobile
                                        stance gun!

P J Littlefield

THEA'S PLACE

I wonder what you are doing now
At this moment, at this hour
Are you having fun
In your garden of heavenly sun?

Do you laugh and leap with joy
Simple pleasures, do you enjoy?
Do you know that you are missed
On your birthday, your photo I've kissed

Whose hand is it that holds you now?
Makes you smile, soothes your brow?
Do you smile as you look down
Or does remembrance bring a frown?

I wish that I could see you grow
Your smiling face I'd love to know
And so I long until the day
That your guiding hand shows me the way.

Emma M Gascoyne

OUR CLIMATE

Our climate is the mixture of the weather we 'enjoy'
From icy blasts in winter to hot summer's sticky cloy,
The rain that falls like stair rods swelling rivers 'til they burst,
Then sun and drought that cracks the lawn you've so long
                                        gently nursed!

The howling gales that strip the blossom rudely from the trees,
Then flatten all the flowers 'til there's nothing left for bees.
The frost that kills the fresh, young shoots just when you thought
                                        they'd set,
And wipes out all your tender plants, when there's no more to get.

Soon comes along a fog, so thick you'd think that it would slice,
And so you drive in second gear - it's then you hit the ice!
That's when you slip, and slide, and waltz along the shining road
To where it's bright and very white - that's when you find it's snowed!

Yet given time the snow will melt, and things won't look so fright'ning,
But no, you got it wrong again, a blinding flash - it's lightning!
And with it, like machine gun fire, the hailstones fly en masse,
They dent your roof, the bonnet too, then smash your windscreen glass.

So now you've sampled everything our climate has in store,
Whatever's next, you won't be shocked, you've seen it all before,
And though you'll travel round the world, and lead a life that's full,
One thing about our *climate* here - it's never, ever dull!

Geoffrey Leech

ONE DAY WILL I EVER BE FAMOUS?

One day will I ever be famous?
Name in lights, lit up in Las Vegas -
I've tried for the last thirty years
To entertain, but it all ends in tears.
I auditioned for 'Opportunity Knocks'
Wearing hot pants and pink spotted socks
But this gawky girl of thirteen -
Failed to impress the late Hughie Green!
As a teenager, I strived hard for fame
Looking for glamour with a showbizzy name.
By the 70s I began doing impressions -
Charging school friends a shilling a session.
Thought I was cool, a dead ringer, so good -
Imitating Frank Spencer, just like Mike Yarwood!
I lapped up the rounds of applause -
Even though, we were behind bedroom doors!
But it never took off - just a phase
The 70s thing - just a craze.
So would I ever become this great star?
Be chauffeured in a limousine car?
In the 80s I applied for 'Page 3'
But they rejected lil' 'ole me -
Said I had two 'underweight' bits -
A polite way of how they put it!
So by the 90s I'm afraid it did seem
Being famous was just a pipe dream.
But in April 2002 -
I wrote poetry out of the blue
Forget now the glamour and glitz
I'll write poems that'll have you in fits.
So maybe I've bided my time -
And I'll make my name writing in rhyme.
Will this be my new claim to fame?
If so - I'm called *Alison Jane.*

Alison Jane Lambert

MARS

A race to reach the planet Mars
our craft to land on Christmas Day.
Mysteriously it has got lost
but one must not forget the USA!

A country that always must be top,
determined to rule the world.
What did they do for us to flop
so stars and stripes could be unfurled?

Their craft landed without a hitch
which really is quite strange,
as Beagle Two sighted its pitch
before their craft was in range!

It travelled millions of miles in space
to discover water and life.
The money spent was a disgrace
considering Earth's problems and strife.

What use is life on Mars to Earth?
What could they with us share?
Such knowledge would be of little worth.
Could we send Earth's starving there?

They've probably viewed us for many years
and have no intentions of being discovered,
seeing Earth they must have many fears
and will never be uncovered.

D Thomas

BLACK DUCKS

One simply must stop
to look at the ducks
on the unmown lawn,
in the grass blades billing,
on little black legs; their
quack: no subtle cowards;
their dynasty: stronger than
strength; this is their task,
their role, keeping simplicity
alive. Downed heads upturn,
smooth as brushed water, to
forage for all ages, no other
job to go to but being.

Wayne David Knoll

THE FRIDAY BAKING SUN

Francis Bacon's in the garden,
Living under a pseudonym.
I'm going under for my sins,
Staying under, christening.
Inhale methane, I feel just swell.
Exhale methane, I'm not too well.

I lost my head, when all around kept theirs
And now I've got no arms to caress
And now I've got no lungs in my chest.
I have got no body.
When I fractured my leg, they came running
But when I cracked my head, they all run in.
Now I've got no legs to rest,
Now I've got no stomach to digest
But I have forgot nobody.

Is there a number I can phone
So I don't have to go through all this on my own?
Where I don't have to feel ashamed,
Because I don't have to leave my name
And I won't have to say it again,
I won't have to say it again.

I'm under the Friday baking sun.
Down at the bottom of Mummy's garden,
Where it feels just like, swimming on land,
If I stop, then I drown.

P J Kemp

MY UNICORN

Where is my unicorn?
The one that looks like Audrey Horne
Aka Sherilyn Fenn
Meeting you would be ultimate zen
The one with fire
Intimate desire
A smile that brings me to silence
Reads my eyes
Sees through my lies
Likes films with a lot of violence
Makes me laugh
Leads me down the right path
As quirky as David Lynch
Dressed to impress
But innocent no less
And reels me in on a winch

Where is my unicorn?
The one who's dressed in all things torn
A scent of lemons and flowers
That keeps me high for hours
Snow-white skin would make her finer
With contrast: red lips and black eyeliner
All these desires are ridiculous wishes
But there must be a goddess amongst all the bitches
I like to set my goals just out of reach
This poor kid would soak up love like a leech

My unicorn like Audrey Horne
Eccentric and beautiful
Witty and wonderful
You'll be the rose and I'll be the thorn
Been thinking about you since I was born
My little honey, my unicorn.

Edward Harvey

A YOB IN PARLIAMENT
(A public opinion)

We have a yob in Parliament
The first in history
And, a member of the Cabinet
Why? Is the biggest mystery
He was once a humble steward
On ships of the Orient Line
As well as annoying passengers
He stirred the union in spare time
Aggression seems his nature
Shown by the swinging of his fist
He thumped a member of the public
While his mind was in a twist
He needs the boot of the British people
To put him in his place
Who is it we refer to?
'The politician with the crab apple face.'

E L Hannam

GRANDAD GREENFINGERS

At last we are getting
Near the end of the year,
We look back on what we've done,
We take stock and have a look
In the mirror.

At last we see
The world as one
And we do not fight
With our sisters and brothers.
When we look at landscapes
And admire the great
Painters of the past
And when love is like a toy room
And a bonfire in November.

Kenneth Mood

SUCH A DEAR - YOU SILLY MAN!

My lovely Californian friend, Pat,
loves our friendly 'chats',
writing daily, via emails,
jokes - gets bored, with all my full details!

We started in 2003 - our great friendship,
it is nice to hear about her and her son, Phillip!
Two sisters and a friendly Alsatian . . .
and learning about America - is such a wonderful education!

Unfortunately she has a poor hand and can't sleep . . .
but said *'She is not ready yet for the scrap heap!'*
Pat daily calls me, *'Such a dear, you silly man!'*
but I hope I am still her No. 1 fan!

When she can, goes to the beach,
which is miles away and out of people's reach!
Pat also likes 'Metallica' - heavy metal band . . .
As she and Phillip, 'air guitar', as they stand!

Have a big hug from me,
if you want more, then ask . . . please!
So Pat, also have some razzle-dazzle,
take care, love Basil!

Barry Ryan

TAKEN FOR GRANTED

There is someone sitting in the chair,
But it feels like there is no one there,
He does not speak to me very much,
I might as well be alone, as such,
Except his socks lie on the floor,
And when I hear his key in the door,
I rush to make a cup of tea,
While he sits and reads his post quietly.
I rustle up a two-course meal,
Even when under the weather I feel,
It would be nice if he showed some concern,
'How was your day?' towards me he'd turn,
A bunch of flowers, a smile and a card,
To show me that he isn't all bad,
A kind word, not a sigh and a frown,
The silence really gets me down,
The telephone bill is very high,
Conversation with others gets me by,
The domestic chores get done by me,
As if by magic, automatically,
I want to shout, 'Please look at me,
I'm a person, a woman,' but he can't see
I have needs and feelings, and I believe,
You must be giving as well as receive,
So remember husbands, alone, feeling low,
A lesson in life. You reap what you sow!

June Melbourn

NORFOLK TEA ROOM

When shopping out in King's Lynn town
I often call to sit me down
At Norfolk Tea Room in that street
That's full of bustling weary feet

The food is very good and filling
Staff, though busy, are always willing
To give attention to each whim
Some fussy people do come in!

Look out the window on the scene
Of people passing, feel serene
Teapots decorate the sill
Just as one hopes they always will

One weekend peace was sadly shattered
Window smashed and vandals scattered
Teapots missing from the sill
Remind me of this evil still

Many tears those nights were shed
The owner could not rest her head
Waiting for a new glass pane
To give her business back again

Now Norfolk Tea Room shines once more
As hungry people find the door
And I am pleased for them to see
That cosy place that pleases me.

Joseph McGarraghy

TAW WHISTLES

Prehistory muddied, their truths not been mute
While hostage; at contact, time starts.
The relics survive onslaughts: whistle and flute,
Their populace dies for the arts.

Taw twee tow, remember the Yanomanno?
Taw twee, I remember them. How?
Taw twee tow, so many like Incan buffalo . . .
Taw twee, I remember them now.

Our best recollections are blurred for these groups
Ascribed now with musical speech.
The music of slaves loops the planet like hoops,
A docile touch faintly a reach.

Descendants of colonists take all they can
In ignorance but with notice.
The musics of genocides coalesce Man:
A traditional healing poultice.

Advanced western thought and their colonists set
Upon Earth their great holy ghost.
These moving dot faces in blood that's still wet
Second our own vision as host.

Some pockets of ethnics perform sacred rites
Like hauling a rock to a spot
With solemn processions, inutile sad plights,
They fight with respect, as they fought.

Amy Alfred Winter

'SHIPS' OF SOCIETY

Leadership:
    In charge and in command,
    it sails at head of fleet,
    its role e'er in demand,
    all challenges to meet.

Comradeship,
    With fellowship abreast
    and friendship on the port,
    with Godspeed they are blest,
    their ventures to support.

Partnership:
    Twin-hulled with double mast,
    Dual-skippered, duties shared.
    Seaworthiness will last
    if skippers rightly paired!

Ownership:
    By ambition we are led,
    with pride, to 'take possession',
    but shipwreck lies ahead
    if 'to own' becomes obsession.

Gamesmanship:
    A crafty craft indeed!
    manoeuvres must be watched.
    Its guile, its tack, its speed
    must be observed - and scotched!
    And of the class above
    One-upmanship appears.
    a vessel few can love;
    is tossed on waves of sneers.

Statesmanship,
> Impressive, stately craft,
> it steers a measured course,
> high profile fore and aft;
> prevails by skill, not force.

Scholarship
> For voyage of discovery,
> exploration and research,
> of past times the recovery,
> of universe the search.

Citizenship:
> There's room for all on board,
> takes pride of place in fleet.
> Warm welcome is assured,
> it's where the 'ships' all meet.

Geoffrey Matthews

A FRIEND WILL ALWAYS BE THERE

A friend will always be there for you, any time of day.
A friend knows what it is you need although you did not say.
She'll be there just to listen when you want to pour things out.
She'll even be there when you feel you need to scream and shout.

A friend will never see you stuck, she'll never let you down.
She'll lift you up in tough times when you feel that you could drown.
For she is there to see you through the good times and the bad,
To laugh when you are happy, to support you when you're sad.

A friend will never judge you like so many others do
And there will never come a time when she's fed up with you.
When things are all against you, on one thing you can depend
The kindness and the loyalty that you get from a friend.

Tina Rose Dolby

A NEW YEAR

As we start another year
Let's remember those we hold dear
Father, mother, sister, brother
Uncles, aunts, grandfather, grandmother
Then our friends from years ago
And new ones we've come to know
The neighbours who have helped us out
We've done the same, that's what life's about
Relatives and friends who have passed away
Remembering them this New Year's Day
We thank the Lord up above
And ask Him to give them our love
We pray that all the wars will cease
And this world will be at peace
We hope that when this year ends
All the countries will be friends
And now it's time to make a start
By wishing everyone peace and happiness from the heart.

Diana Daley

SUN IN THE BLUE

Sun in the blue,
Where are you?

Time on my hands,
For loving you.
Always waiting for,
The sun in the blue.

In loving you,
What have I done?
To be without pain,
When will this time come?

Time on my hands,
What can I do?
I need to find,
The sun in the blue.

From my head to my heart,
I'm empty of belief.
What have I done,
To be living in this grief?

Innocent but guilty,
I fell into the trap.
Imprisoned by love,
Became more than a mishap.

Give it to me,
The sun in my eyes.
Release me, it's time,
To see those blue skies.

Show it to me,
Make me anew.
Let me start over,
Give me the sun in the blue.

Sun in the blue,
What did I do?
Where are you?

Carol Ann Darling

WHILE YOU WERE SLEEPING

A shaft of moonlight broke away, and crept
beneath the close-drawn curtain folds.
Forgetting my desire to sleep,
I marvelled at your features as you slept.
The moonbeam stray had bathed them in a glow,
a sheen, cold as the marble knights
reclining in eternal rest,
cathedral-tombed from centuries ago.
But low and gentle, steady breathing told me
your temples would be warm to touch;
your slumber but a night-long span.
At daybreak you will wake, arouse and hold me.

Valerie Calvert

ANOTHER DAY OVER

Sometimes the hours pass so slowly
You wonder if the day will ever end,
When the clock face appears static
The time to come is not your friend.

Are the hands turning backwards
Or are they frozen in a time vault?
When you wish for the hours to fly,
It looks like they have come to a halt.

Yet, each tick of the clock is heard
So you can tell, that this is no lie,
Thus the minutes ebb away quietly
And true time will pass by and by.

The end of day will surely happen
There is no sense in feeling shame,
You cannot stop time, time is time
And time will be another day again.

George S Johnstone

I Felt An Angel's Breath

Cooling winds steadily blow across town.
Trees wave goodbye where the sun goes down
Yet night breezes still linger over dark eerie land
Like delicate fingers on an outstretched hand
Bright stars suddenly appear,
Chilly silent world stands still
Upon midnight air comes icy breath
Passing o'er grey skies,
Music numbs sweet ghostly echoes,
They had bade him sleep.
They bring Heaven's last lonely haunting lament
For every joy that passes
Something beautiful shall always remain.

Ann Hathaway

MIXING A CHRISTMAS RECIPE

Start by taking out the pips of hatred
Then take a pinch of sweet happiness and sieve out the grains of war
Mix in Christmas cheer and goodwill,
This should take away the taste of despair.

Put in snow, presents and parties straight out of the can
Pick out the pips of evil, which are very deadly,
Cook for an hour or two then decorate with lights and holly
That will make a perfect Christmas pud.

Sean Hines (11)

CHINESE BOWLER MAN

I saw an old man, a Chinese man
    rolling and bowing with pleasure,
All on his own he strolled round the green
    glancing and watching the weather.
He would stop for a moment and probably ponder
    to see if his eye was straight,
The bowl left his hand and shot out in front
    but missed the final bait.
Slow was his pace, he gathered his bowls
    ready to try once more,
This time the Jack flew into the ditch
    so stamped his wee feet on the floor.
I took one last look faced with farewell
    to see him calmly move,
This sweet Chinese man, cap all askew
    was wearing a pair of odd shoes.

Suzzette Goddard

HUMANITY

We were given this Earth,
For us to live upon,
But it doesn't seem long,
Until all will be gone,

Man has the theory
That one should rule all,
Destroying each other,
Till all will fall,

Let's live in peace,
And share this gift,
Stop all the war,
It's time to shift,

So all can enjoy,
The award of life,
Without any pain,
Or any great strife.

Alan Gordon

THE TRUE AMERICANS

These Indian tribes had the freedom as they rode the ranges
They believed in Manitou, the spirit of fighting braves
This mighty warrior, some had a sighting, this guardian of plains
In his hands he held tight to his steed's cloud-like reins

Upon the high mountains, 'Many Chiefs', his hands were raised
in prayers
Then he called upon Great Manitou to ride with them on their
battle days
This is a well-known legend, the chief said he would face their foes
This beautiful magnificent figure and mount shone in an awesome
ghostly glow.

They said he was the guardian of the rivers, the mountains and
the plains
That the Great White Spirit would come to protect them all again
The beautiful white mount would silently neigh, his hooves would
quietly prance
Around those large totem poles, the painted braves began their
war dance.

These cruel hunters would slaughter the buffalo for their meat
and hides
These vile white men emptied the plains where the herds roamed
the countryside
Then those greedy miners would destroy the land for the gold
they craved
They would violate the tribes and their sacred burial graves.

These white people would cross the plains in their vast wagon trains
The beautiful high mountain forests would cry in murderous pain
They murdered these proud people and destroyed the Indian nations
These tribes were enslaved, their vile prison was a reservation.

J F Grainger

SEASON FOR A KING

If nobody loves you
and your heart is sinking low,
tell yourself it isn't so!
Think on days of youth and love,
let wild imagination flow,
and water will change to wine
when you gaze into the sky
and see God's face divine.
Listen to the bluebirds sing.
Awaken your heart,
here comes the spring,
the season for a king.
Feed the pure white swans today
down along the harbour bay,
and water will change to wine
when you gaze into the sky
and see God's face divine.

Joyce Hemsley

MY SOULMATE
(For Rhona)

I'm sitting here thinking of the things I have done
the times that were hard and the times I had fun,
I wish I could talk to you about this
as you'd understand and that's what I miss.

I feel I am reliving your life,
the problems you've had, the troubles and strife
it has been hard, I've been there too
and that's why I feel I can relate to you.

Both our childhoods were painful, you see
and that's why I feel you would understand me,
if only I had the chance to tell you
about the events I went through too.

If we met, you'd realise how similar we are
but you've made your life, you've become a star,
at least we both believe in fate
and maybe in you I'll find my soulmate.

Rachael Ford

SUMMER SERENITY

Waves crawling along the coast,
White sand shimmering in the bright sun,
Fishing boats gliding across the sea,
This is the summer serenity.

Pale, fluffy clouds floating in the firmament,
Seagulls soaring about the subterranean ocean,
Fish swimming gracefully,
This is the summer serenity.

Dolphins leaping in and out of the water,
Seaweed reaching out of the rock pools,
Kites in the zephyr, swaying merrily,
This is the summer serenity.

Mrinalini Dey

I'M SORRY

I'm sorry we had to part.
I'm sorry that I let you break my heart.
I'm sorry I gave my love so true to you.
I'm sorry you said what you did.
I'm sorry I let you know my feelings.
I'm sorry for being a fool.
I'm sorry that I fell for you.
I'm sorry for letting you have a laugh on me.
I'm sorry our romance was not to be.
I'm sorry for you're the loser, not me.

Norman Andrew Downie

THE LAST DAY

We kissed and cuddled and said our goodbyes
As Jack went through the door
Because we knew we were not going
To see him anymore
He lay on the floor day after day
His quality of life just faded away
After a time poor Jack went blind
And became disorientated in his mind
We had Jack for six long years
And when he went, our eyes were wet with tears
Poor Anna, his loyal and trusty friend
Loved him right to the very end
Though our hearts were full of grief
No more pain was a happy relief
Now poor Jack has now sadly gone
But the memory of Jack in our minds lives on.

Bert Booley

FOUNDATIONS

My mind looks back to a gentler age,
To an era I have not known,
Where life as we know it was yet to be,
But the seeds of today were sown.
When folk were inclined to reminisce
And reflect on the simpler things,
To pluck a daisy, to smell a red rose,
Marvel at a butterfly's wings.

The seasons come and the seasons go
And time moves relentlessly on,
But spare a thought for those gone ahead
And their lives before they were done.
Without these more humble, gentler folk,
Where would we be today?
It takes time to fashion a masterpiece
From a piece of unmoulded clay.

Patricia Adele Draper

OF ROYALTY

King and Queen of this court
Their prince had to sort
For a lesson on him was taught
The poor lad had been caught.

Michael D Bedford

WHISTLING

Where have all the whistlers gone;
that were heard in days gone by?
Have people really lost the knack,
or perhaps, don't even try?

Errand boys and paper boys,
all whistled on their rounds,
but now - today, in London,
you rarely hear the sound.

Along with smiling faces,
whistlers are but few;
I suspect the world we now live in,
might give us all a clue.

Murders, mayhem, terrorism, wars,
comprise most daily news;
not much to smile or whistle about,
and that's my honest view.

So, will we ever hear again,
whistling, throughout our land,
or has it gone forever;
by the EU, even banned!

Peter Mahoney

THE PATH

Our life is already mapped out for us
But we choose which way we want to go
But do we really, really know?
We either follow the path that's there
Or sometimes do we really care?
Or go off the rails
Following sand and sails
Take an adventure,
Take a chance
Take the risk
Or do we stick to the rigid road
Be as good as we've been told
Maybe make life much easier?
But where's the fun without a challenge
We have a choice
We do what we want
But is it always good for us, or even right?
Well, we won't know, we need to learn
The hard way only gives discern
So keeping to the path is an easier option
If we only knew which path to take!
An easier life that we can make.
Can it be for our own sake.

T Hartley

EPISTLE TO D I BRIAN TUCKWOOD

For lies spoken
Nerves broken

Looking in the mirror
At twisted figure

Horns on your head
As you sleep in bed

Protection from the top
Will not stop

You being judged
From Almighty above.

John McCartney

A MAGICAL STARRY NIGHT

On a magical starry night,
I have heard the moon will start to fall,
Fairies will ride on the stars this night,
Listen carefully, you may hear them call.

On a magical starry night,
When only dew falls to the ground,
Fairies dance and weave with delight,
Casting shapes and patterns all around.

On a magical starry night,
People gaze and are aware,
Of words being written by the stars,
Saying, 'Let there be peace on Earth everywhere.'

Harriet Elizabeth Hobbs (11)

TO LOOK INTO MY EYES

I long for a baby to hold in my arms,
Each time I try it's like sand flowing through my palms.
Once, twice and three times I have tried,
Every time I cried.
Why is hard to want to be a mum?
To have children running around,
Making loud noises and banging on drums.
People dream of having big families too,
I dream of having one to make my dream come true.
If I only knew the reason why,
Why do my babies have to die?
I pray to the Lord to give me the strength,
To keep trying and to go to all the lengths,
To make me strong and find out why,
If I give up now I will never know why.

Maggie Hickinbotham

IN SEARCH OF JORDAN MURDOCK (AGED 14 YEARS)

From a crowded shoreline
Its community in shock
Searching through the waves
The eyes and voices of Killough

Swallowed by a hungry sea
Upon a bitter day
A young boy who had gone
Along the quay with friends, to play

In the air and on the water
Many men set course
To pierce the sea's defiant surface
Battle with its force

Torch lights shone to guide his body
And his spirit home
Whilst in amongst the rocks
And through the seaweed folks would comb

Desperation hailed the sun
It struggled with the moon
Saw prayers all floating Heavenwards
'Please, let us find him soon!'

But echoes through the harbour still
The last words this child spoke
'I love you . . .' as his grip
Upon this mortal world was broke.

Kim Montia

THE ARMED FORCES

Armed Forces went to occupy
Sent in by a politician's lie
Sent here, sent there, sent almost anywhere

Raise the flag of unity
Trying to form a community

Too many factions, too many distractions
Too many prediction, too many contradictions

Wipe your blood from your uniform
These people just won't conform

I ain't mocking, you do a fine job
Where you go is not your fault
Obeying orders is your vocation
Sent abroad, it's your occupation

Fine discipline to every man
It's not the generals who carry the can
Leave the problem at the politicians' door
That is what they are paid for.

I'm not perfect but I know the score!

Brian Lunt

COMFORT

She wraps it around her little fingers.
She toddles round with it, trailing behind her.
Like a ghost monster chasing, or a swan's wing
fluttering lightly; it gets caught and tugs her.
She cries, she cannot retrieve it; it snaps loose,
she's happy and cuddles it.

She's tired, so lies down on the sofa awhile.
She wraps it around her fingers,
it's soft and fluffy.
She strokes her face with it,
it's safe and warm.
She likes the smell of it,
it's light and snugly.

She sucks it a while, 'Urgh,' she groans,
then continues to stroke her face.
'Ohhh,' she sighs, 'it's wet and it's soggy.'
She turns it round and buries into it,
with a happy smile.
She sleeps now, safe and sound.

Linda Pickering

CHOICE - PART 1

Please believe, take heed
This is (almost) all the advice you'll ever need
Please take heed, from this chain of troublesome traits
Which could bring about your traumatic fate
It'll be hard if you're ever entangled in one mangled link
But 'Much Luck,' here's hoping you don't sink . . .
Rumours lead to traumas, then desperation hits you
As you try to reclaim the pieces cut adrift
Desperation leads to depravation, as your ideals shift
Then your loneliness enforces paranoia
Paranoia, temptation, condemnation, rejection, scrambling
Soul-searching, hoping, choking, provoking
Swaying, praying, repetitive cycle of recyclable doom
A bond of doom which *can* and *must* be *smashed!*
Insult, broken heart, unyielding routine
Cynicism, bitterness, self-harm, charm, smarm, broken arm!
Planning, learning, yearning, churning, burning
Not a solitary choice
Climbing, hiding, chiming, confiding
Resting, testing, stalling, falling, lying, crying
It should be your choice
Clambering, losing, bruising, cruising
Some higher state, *give them a voice!*
Just floating, treading water, swimming or drowning?
On the block or holding the axe?
Content with the jagged surface, or fill in the cracks?
If your head rolls, then let it chatter on to a mesmerised crowd
Let your legacy's link be firm, like *Queen Mary's* when bowed
On the block or holding the axe?
Content with the jagged surface, or fill in the cracks?
Believe me . . .
If any of these haunting traits creep up on you
Beware, take all the possible precautions
If it's too late, then forget it . . .
Idiots!

Simon Cardy

A NAME IN A CROWD

In the cells of learning where Oxford's knowledge grows,
In the city of spires where the Isis flows,
A poet.
Yes! The Warrior Poet is born,
In the January snows on the Eights (eighth?) one early morn,
If you've never heard of him,
This is your chance,
'Eamon John Healy' will lead you in a dance,
Haunted by the poets! Who long before him -
Died,
The Warrior Poet will dance by your side,
Some call me crazy - others say that I'm insane,
But I am the Warrior Poet! Now please remember my name,
Down Long Wall kicking tin cans,
Up the Cowley Road - BMW is at the top,
Oxford City is still like a beautiful shroud,
Moving silently in a crowd,
Covered in cobwebs, limping cripples pass by,
The seat of learning makes a poet cry,
Melting the steel crumbling the bones of the dead,
Barbed wire is enclosed around Oxford's soul,
Students are naked running for buses, double-deckers,
In Iffly Road, some just post a letter,
Down St Ebbs the drunks swim in their sick,
Sumertown and Cutteslow,
I call home,
Me,
The Warrior Poet out on my own.

Eamon John Healy - The Warrior Poet

THIS LAND

People wander around this Earth,
like sheep in their flocks
drifting from place to place,
people of no importance,
people of no worth,
homeless and helpless,
no country on Earth.

No place to go to take off their shoes,
no place to go for the children to sleep,
they wander from year to year,
never to find any land to keep,
never a place to call a home,
in thousands they wander all alone.

Their tears are silent
their words are not heard,
their pain is deep as they drift
starving upon this Earth,
is this land not big enough
for the Muslims and the Serbs?
For the Chechnians and the Russians
and no room for the Kurds?
Is this land not big enough to live without the wars?
To live with peace and happiness
let's open up our doors.

Dianne Audrey Daniels

UNTITLED

I read the morning paper with a cup of tea,
And a pair of boobs spoke to me,
Saying, 'All day long when you're out,
Strange things will happen round about.'

Someone pumped next to me,
I heard it shout, 'Whey-hey, I'm free.'
Nobody else heard it yell,
But I saw it ringing a doorbell.

A dog in a park done a poo,
Wiped its bum, no one knew,
The jobby got up and ran away,
That's not a sight you see every day.

I saw the pump later that day,
Talking to the jobby that ran away,
Talking about a bit of a do
Their local night club, the public loo.

Next morning, with the paper and a cup of tea
The headlines jumped out at me,
I started to laugh with what I knew,
Gas movements close public loo.

Dale Finlay

A Poem For Ariana

Another year has gone by, and how you have grown,
from a quaint little girl to one with a mind of her own.

How you have progressed through life's ups and downs,
new strength you have been given,
of that I am proud.

So proud of the fact that you are my daughter,
no better a friend I could have,
may you grow with much love and laughter,
on your road of happiness.

Pauline Chiarelli

THE VOICE IN MY HEAD

I sat in the corner, scared and cold,
The voices were hurting my head,
Each noise like an echo, surrounding my mind,
The sounds of the things that I dread.

Make them go, can't take much more,
Why is this happening to me?
I'm sick of this life of torture and pain,
What can I do to be free?

Want out of this mess, just want to escape,
For things to be normal again,
Get rid of the scars, get rid of the pills,
Be happy for once now and then.

So why do I smile when the cut is so deep?
When all I can see is the blood?
The thought makes me shiver but not from the cold
The feeling I got was so good.

This voice that took over my thoughts once again,
The one that is making me cry
'Cut deeper,' it said, 'and then it will end.
And then I will leave you to die.'

Samantha Walsh

BLACK SILK

The moon settles on the night,
The death of day,
The fading light.
As flowers close
And hide their beauty,
Silks of darkness
Rest upon the stillness
And an eerie silence
Fills the air.
Sudden is the abandonment,
As alone I wait
For the crossing of time,
To meet the celestial dawn.

Sue Umanski

TO THE MAN I'VE ALWAYS LOVED

To the man - I've always loved,
To the man - I always will.
To the man - who is my friend,
   And my lover till the end.

To the man - I love so much,
To the man - whose lovely touch,
   Flames my heart, my body and soul,
To the man - whose love I stole.

To the man - whose body is warm and inviting,
To the man - who makes love so wild and exciting.
To the man - I adore, forever and more,
To the man - who makes life, worth living for.

To the man - whose love, makes me feel so great,
To the man - I can trust, my soulmate.
To the man - who gives, all his time and affection,
To the man - who is, the very heart of perfection.

S Longford

BE GOD FOR THE DAY

Lots of gases in old glass jars
God made man on Earth, moon and Mars.
Did you know all kinds He did make
From that worm that crawls out of a lake
It was the hardest job He could do
Think to yourself, if you're making you.
If you sat for ten million years
Would you find two great dishes for ears?
Take a look at secret agents and spies
And find two video cameras for your eyes.

If I were maybe a Russian defector
Who for a nose made a smoke detector.
Build a large factory in the deep south
Where food you test for the man's mouth.
To save energy in a battery loss aggravation
You would need a very large power station.
Ten miles of pipes to take the waste
Join to the mouth factory there to taste.
You need a mile-high computer for the brain
Run a sewer across country, water to drain.

Into you fill ten tons of giant pills
Make it move on a long row of wheels.
You would at least get a slow motion
If two should meet you've got a commotion.
From the sea you reclaim all the land
Get two great cranes to use as hands
Into the mouth put a tape for the voice
Any tongue can be your own choice.
Each would build in his own sweet way
Now you've been God for the day.

Colin Allsop

THE FUTURE NOW

As you watch outdated films
with outdated modes of fight
the warlords visited me in flight
on the computer where I live in the lab.

My co-ordinates are given out
for worldwide students whom your taxes pay
torture on the keyboard at the lab and play
on the computer which is also me.

Every word I use, yes, think and paint
appears on the computer already printed and the private
lab friends come and use it all as their own, paid
sponsored by the State by your taxes.

They practise on remedials now us
kill anyone and all, I'd rather not tell
this lab boss has killed at least twelve
academics, artists and destroyed twenty families by herself.

Finally they mashed the arm on my right
now see if you can write
so I send you this as a dissident with a glove
fled from the country we so admired and helped to rebuild.

As you watch outdated films
the computer where I live in the lab
reaches its sound corridors ranging across the globe
after twenty years, still a prisoner

Even here!

Renate Fekete

Scoop!

Excuse me a minute - I must see what is in it
It is something that I should learn,
I will bear and grin it - why in that manger bin it?
Goodness gracious, it is a newborn bairn,
It I must smother - where is the mother? -
This is something that does seem grand,
Virgin Mother! - Excuse my laughter -
Is this something that the good Lord planned?
Your name is *Mary!* - Boy this is scary -
I did not know it was you standing there,
A mite too hairy - tell me Mary - what will become of it -
Or don't you really care?
I am a reporter - perhaps I shouldn't oughta -
If I am intruding, please I forgive,
I *will* be loyal - I am a 'Royal' -
Here are some presents that I should give,
I *will* tell the story - claim the glory -
All our readers will go bonkers over this,
The tale telling stop him yelling -
Why don't you give him a slobbering kiss?
Read my paper about this caper -
A mother who is both meek and mild,
I can see the headline - it will suit fine -
'Virgin Mary has a fatherless child.'
Sorry, if offended, my notes are ended -
I promise to be a decent male,
She was *pregnant* without an *entrant!* -
Thousands will read it so it cannot fail,
Bye-bye darling - you look charming -
I will do whatever you like,
That's underhanded - scoop abandoned -
As I have been speared through - by a *lightning strike!*

Jon El Wright

MY LOVELY MUM

My lovely mum,
For me she does care,
Every day she fills my tum,
Right till I'm full - fair and square.

My lovely mum,
Serves vegetables - raw,
When she says, 'Oh crumb!'
I know it's time for me to close the door.

My lovely mum,
Makes me laugh,
As she's full of fun,
And she's the best mother and a half.

My lovely mum,
Who I drive up the wall,
Says, 'Stop it my sugar plum,
Let's not fight, shout or scream at all.'

My lovely mum,
Reminds me to never forget her special day,
Where I sing and hum,
Wishing her a 'Happy Mother's Day'!

Hartinajit Kaur Dulay (12)

ANARCHY IN THE UK

Anarchy in the UK.
Let's protest against our government,
believe me it'll be okay
so let's kill the Queen.

Let's riot
and cause mass destruction,
let's rape the priests
and see how they feel about it.

How about ripping off the social?
Why not?
They can afford it,
let's all strip naked
and flash our arses.

Let's vandalise the police stations
and call them 'pigs',
let's support the IRA
and help them destroy this nation!

Chris T Barber

THE LAST WILL AND TESTAMENT OF REX KING

This is the last will and testament of me, Rex King,
please no tears, as I can't stand that sort of thing,
of sound mind and sound body, so my doctor said,
which obviously isn't true, then why is *this* being read?
To my special mother, Eloise, who I hope isn't too sad,
here for you, is 14 million pounds, for meeting my dad,
for my wonderful father, George, funny as it sounds,
here for you, from me, is *another* 14 million pounds!
To my son, Alex, who has a roving eye for loose women,
if he settles down, my French chateau, can have him in,
to my daughter, Sue, a proud lesbian, totally unmanned,
six million pounds if she raises a family with a husband,
and to the 'friend' of Sue, who I only ever met twice,
a one-way cruise to New Zealand, cheap at the price,
to my second son, Nick, a lazy, scruffy, boozy layabout,
get a job, two million pounds, if he gets his finger out,
to my youngest daughter, Athena, so dull and so plain,
six million pounds, as I gave her such a stupid name,
to my youngest son, Toby, who said with money I was tight,
I give absolutely nothing, as in your case, son, you are right!
To my best friend, Bob, who was only ever sober rarely,
a crate of alcohol-free lager, although it tastes like pee,
to my first wife, Rona, who was always a right little raver,
something battery-operated, and it's *not* an electric shaver,
to my nephew, Joe, who with his wife *so* wants a son,
12 months supply of Viagra, and next year, another one,
and finally the remainder of my considerable estate,
to the great love of my life forever, and my best mate,
for the last 10-or-so minutes in bed, my wife, Grace,
who brought on my heart attack in the first place!

Christopher Higgins

AFRICAN BLUSH

Africa, my Africa
Homeward enchanting maybe
Snow mountains
Drawn over with sweet lace
Cloud capturing
The sky's tender grace
In awe moving across vast plains
Lightly wild and gentle
Hand-crafted landscape
Picture design carved by the mantle
Only true spirit
Creature of the safari game
Fast, full of freedom
To us exquisite features by name
Pumping hearts
Nature's cost never tame
Golden and bronzed their shadows
Magnificent colours to blame
Standing still
Hearts beating, drums inside the flame
Exploding spheres
The lovers' past kiss never rushed
Plucked with care
The flower, an African blush.

Jan Ross

MANY MORE...

Once, I cried a tear
It fell upon the snow
I beheld an angel in its path
A glistening, golden glow

I prayed upon the sunset
With the wind upon my soul
Sat until the air was cold
And grew, so gracefully old

Once, I stopped a raindrop
From smashing on the ground
I caught it upon my open palm
With a wonderful bouncing sound

I lay upon the soaked grey floor
And saved the lives, of many more . . .

Jodi Wheeler

MOTHER'S DAY

My mum cares and loves in every way
She does her best every day.
She pays for what she uses
And what she loses.

She can get very cross
When my sister wants to be the boss.
When she's got a test
She always wants a rest.

My mum likes to have fun
And she always likes to go for a run
She takes us on day trips
Then she likes to have a long kip.

My mum can be very lazy
Then she starts to go crazy
She can be very nasty
Then makes us some pasties.

Karandip Kaur Dulay (10)

UNTITLED

Food on the table
Water in the tap
Born in a stable
With feathers in his cap.

P Allen

DANDELION SCULPTURE

Dandelion sculpture,
Moon happy shadow,
Blue above pageant,
Flower almost,
Summer swallow sky,
Morning surprise,
Red sun murmur,
Rise and wander,
Holiday thought,
Beautiful between beneath.

Allan Pow

PIE IN THE SKY

The lover's palette, is the moon on high,
His words, his oils, to make her sigh.
He paints his pictures of love, to swoon,
Knowingly using his asset the moon.

Her heart he steals, with a few moonbeams,
As he colourfully sketches, fulfilment of dreams.
But what if fulfilment, not her sole need?
Reproductive urges, she needs to feed.

The lover now cornered, who's fooling who?
It's not so clever, when they control you.
All of the pictures, you paint at the start,
Should come from the mind, not of the heart.

Sid De Knees

NEVER DECEIVING AND NEVER DECEIVED

Blessed be seemingly impossible dreams!
Dreams, not of Utopia, of a better world!
A kinder world, altogether more gentle,
Where the glamorisation of violence
Falls on deaf ears and blind eyes.
A world where none of us shrink from
Naming evil: facing up to eradicating it;
Not ignoring it and refusing to discuss it!
Where a murderer's smooth talk
Falls on deaf ears and blind eyes!
A place where deaf folk want to listen,
Blind people see just what love endures
That cannot be concealed behind lies
Skilfully told by those with most to lose
Should truth ever rear its ugly head!
Truth is self-contained, obviously so
When perceived by those who hunger
And thirst after righteousness.
How much do you hunger and thirst
After righteousness, or don't you care?
Seek ye first the real within
Where love, light and peace dwell,
Then all good things are added
In due season.
Evil casts a long shadow across truth
Hidden deep in the shadows
Where God sees it all too clearly.
It pains Him that liars love Him not
As His love reaches equally - to all.

Jesu Ah'so

WERE I TO MEET A WIZARD

Were I to meet a wizard
Who would kindly say to me?
'Be what you like for a day'
Do you know what I'd be?
I'd be a skylark
I'd fly away over the park
And I'd sing, and I'd sing and I'd sing.
Then I'd call on Mr King,
King's my boss
His motto is 'profit not loss'
His sad mind's on money,
He can't see life's funny.
I'd sing, 'Mr King, give money away,
Mr King, life's gay
Money weighs you down,
Gives you a terrible frown.
I'm not your little clerk,
I'm now a bright skylark,
Sing, Mr King, sing.'

Mary Frances Mooney

POSTCARDS

Postcards from our holidays
Funfairs, a sunny haze
Telling how wonderful our time spent
But this postcard can't be sent, not by Royal Mail
It needs to be heaven's angels, retail
You see it's for my nan
Who no longer can
Collect Royal Mail
She died, you see, weak and frail
Can you send my nan this card
For I know you could find it hard?
Could you try and send a word
Tell Nan how we're doing, I know it's absurd?
It's the only mail, we want to send
Just a message for Gran, my best friend
Now she's gone, from earthly sight
Do you think you could send her this card
Even though it might seem hard?
I need to tell her, I love her so
That's where I need my postcard to go
To my dear nan, if you can,
Let her know I'm here,
And that I love her dear
Just let me see that smile on her face
Can't send it first class
I don't know how to reach Heaven alas
It needs to be sent 'special delivery'
A postcard full of love from little Marie
Just to say, 'Hello Nan, how are you?'
Please send it, I pray that you do.

Tracey Marie

SORELY MISSED

I stand on the hill
and I see the girl from home.
Visualise her bright smile
and ever shining eyes

A lot of footsteps
have crossed the path since then
I wish her hand were here now
to give me courage and strength

No fear lived in me then
though I'd hate to see
a tear on her face;
forever chasing laughter

Through mists of time
escape the crying rain
now walk bravely forward
to slaughter my modern-day demons.

Jeff Brooks

DON'T UNDERESTIMATE THE COLOUR RED

The long wide road of lost hope
Yawns at its lost once-worldy power
Left a second-rater fighting from the bottom up
Scratching at granite walls with bleeding fingers
Screaming at
New invention, a fear of change

Yet look! There are New Russians touched by Midas
Who tear and rip at old orders
Move their mice to foreign sites
Play the field of sleeping Americans
To show
Who rules this crime-filled planet.

Ian Bowen

I STAND ALONE

I stood alone 'neath milk-white cloud,
I stood alone and cried aloud,
No battles here, nay won or lost.
No one to grieve or count the cost.

I stood alone near rippling stream,
With water fresh, and pure, and clean.
Meandering through a valley green.

I stood alone by a river clear,
And countless beasts then did appear,
On seeing me, they showed no fear.

I stood alone on a mountain high,
Whose towering pinnacles kissed an azure sky
And doves of peace were flying by.

I stood alone near rolling sea,
Where majestic whales knew nought of me
And all the creatures of the deep at peace I see.

I stood alone but now it seems,
I stood alone just wrapped in dreams.

L Baynes

THE PROPOSAL OF MARRIAGE

My love is so powerful,
That I can never leave you,
I've been awake all last night,
Scared and worried too.

You are the one,
The one that I love,
Through over a year,
It's never gone.

It's only one little word,
That can change our lives
Please say yes,
My love divine.

Will you marry me?

Steven Borysewicz

LOSS LEADERS

Why can't we have simple prices?
Ev'ry shopping day's a crisis.
Two for one; this week it's butter.
Next week I'll beg, in the gutter!
Keep the coupon, when I choose it,
Fifty pence if I don't lose it.
Win a house, a car, a phone.
Why can't they leave me alone?
Shall I buy a piece of steak?
Can't! It's doubled since last week!
Need a mind like a computer.
Whose idea? I think I'll shoot her.
At the checkout, 'Have you got a
Card for points?' I wish I'd shot her!

John Belcher

A DANCE OF TIME

Fast whirling thoughts rear
Feelings that I hold so dear.
With longing, hope and fear
Twirling events, making the past wear'.
Somehow the jigging of mind,
Makes my feet want to dance I find.
Only age slows me down, how unkind,
Thinking back to times, I did unwind.
The pinnacle of all this prancing,
Gone with the passage, enhancing
Memories long gone, dancing,
My mind recalling and romancing.

Marj Busby

THE BUFFALO

With beards just like the frozen snow
Onward, onward, onward go
Across the plain
The buffalo.

David A Bray

AXE THE TV LICENCE FEE!
(The Daily Express Crusade)

Axe the TV licence fee!
Let's end this gross monopoly
That yearly takes its grievous toll!
Its head deserves to rock and roll!
Let's stop the rot, the waste, the trash!
Let's quit the parting of our cash!
Let's keep our money safe and sound!
Let's cut the cords by which we're bound!
What rights have they to all our dough
And what allegiance do we owe?
Millions here and millions there?
A travesty beyond compare!
Each VCR and TV owned
Has legal rules such that we groaned,
For by the law the Beeb gets pay!
Axe the licence, without delay!
Destroy it! Stop it! End this 'tax'!
Together, let's all swing the axe!
It's long past due! No need to vote!
God bless the crusade! Blair, take note!

D K F Martindale

STREAM

Have you ever stood by a tree
And watched the stream flow by?
Where are you meandering to?
Are my thoughts as you go by

Do you see the paper boats
With messages inside?
Or do you tickle the fish
As you go on your way?

Do you see the larks
As their wings cast a shadow
Across your silver stream
As you flow on by?

I wonder if you see
The foxes and the badgers
At dusk as they drink
From your crystal stream?

And can you see me
Standing by the willow tree
Watching the stream
As you pass by me?

R Mills

Untitled

It seems like only yesterday when we were having fun,
going to the cinema, or strolling in the sun.
Time passed by, the children came,
bringing lots of joy,
with the wondrous look on every face,
as they played with each new toy.
As years roll on, time takes its toll,
our chicks have left their nest.
But there this story does not end,
for you must hear the rest.
Our grandchildren, girls and boys,
excited over *their* new toys,
full of vigour, full of zest, this is what
we're living for.
Before in peace we rest.

Edward Hill

THE TAURUS MAN

When the feelings have gone and you want me no more,
You were the one I chose to adore,
And when my face is so far from your mind,
I loved you unconditionally and life is unkind,
And when my life is ebbing away,
I will be able honestly to say,
I loved you each new dawning day,
No one could be more happy than me,
When wrapped in your arms where I longed to be,
If only the Taurus Man could truly love me,
My life would have been perfect but only for me,
But I can dream of what cannot be,
The Taurus Man said he was not for me.

Ellen Chambers

UNDERGRADUATES UNDERGROUND

travelling on the bakerloo (catching trains in the rain),
sidling onwards two by two (it's madness underground).
there flows one man with a beard, here a girl in beaded gear,
(in dirtied sweaters they appear). undergraduates underground.

smoking wacky substances (choking in urinal pits),
with burnt-on hair, they pit their wits
with the city sounds,
subjugated, peasy brains, interpity student veins (haversacks
of cheap-rape pain). undergraduates underground.

there goes one with bags of time (scooting-up, he's refined),
here's another boozing slime (a parlatan defamed).
men with books and broken spines (wafer-thin, easy minds),
mobile menaces in rhyme. undergraduates underground.

late at night they come from pubs (fluking-up, praised by god),
from the buildings on the hills (learning places, always ill),
they exude their student will,
p****d as farts, bold as nails (drowning in a glass of ale),
roundabouted, going stale. undergraduates underground.

they confess to one-night stands (beaten up, condoms bang),
and they writhe in broken cars (eaten up, axles jar).
though they be our futures now (pageless kids, golden boughs),
they begin the trends of power, undergraduates underground.

coughing up tubercular sums, (camden market bass and drum),
eating lentils off a bed (carried off before they're wed),
standing with credential frowns,
poisily in paper crowns (raucous giggles in a mound),
they roll idly out of bounds. undergraduates underground.

John Delaney

SEPTEMBER ELEVEN

Today the world remembers, today the world stood still
      And thoughts of love, and memories
Return in spite of years, they did not die this awesome day,
      There was no time to kneel and pray
For evil, swift and silent came.
      With beliefs abundant, yet full of shame

This day the world remembers, those so truly brave
      Their actions so unselfish, their lives they readily gave
The years pass by so quickly, may heal the broken hearts,
      Will make us feel quite humble, to make another start

Twin Towers, so majestic, reaching for the sky
      But they are never nearer Heaven, as life goes swiftly by
The stairs, the lifts, the mobile phones, all had a part to play
      When those three words *I love you*
With so little time to say, but life goes by, as tears run dry
      Never must we forget, live on young love
And those in Heaven, remember this day for always
      That fateful nine eleven.

E F Croker

JOURNEY'S END

How long will I have to journey when I pass over
To get to the higher realms to the class,
The class of scholars who is above
Because they've showered blessings and your love,

Oh, Lord, show me the way to repent
For all the sins I have not seen in my life,
Abandoning my children and my wife,

Please Lord, forgive my abusive ways
And shower me with your beautiful days,
For I want to follow you in my future lives
Make me a busy bee in your hall of hives.

So that I may give what you have taught
Love in abundance for man and child,
And make me your servant for evermore
So that I can pass through that golden door,

For I know my thoughts were all of money
But I'd sooner have real love which makes honey
Then maybe when my time comes, I'll be forever your slave.

M J Chadwick

CLEVER

Bullies think they are so clever,
Picking on people no matter the weather,
We should stand together,
Sticking up for ourselves is hard to do,
But a little love will get us through,
So go away bullies, we won't cry, boo-hoo!

Jackie Jones-Cahill

THE LINES OF LIFE

The lines of life they twist and curve,
Or go straight for a while then suddenly swerve,
Some form a circle or maybe a square,
Some are real heavy and some aren't quite there,
Some form wild pictures others quite tame,
But nobody's lines are ever the same.

Jay Berkowitz

FULLY BOOKED INSANIA

We built a history that fitted the picture whatever the mixture.
Like a shelf full of different books we undertook to combine
them into one.
So when we found the space capsule our scientists explained it.
Without a doubt this container came from another planet.
Had there been another explanation heaven knows it couldn't be found.
Yet had we just been able to separate the facts.
Thinking though as we did, to be on page 50 of Earth's only history,
Put us about a billion light years from the truth.
The fact was our astronaut wasn't alien but human
He actually came from a previous incarnation of our Earth page 82.
From a dead launch funeral, by a people that sought to save their world
With a sacrificial space corpse.
True, very true and not for the first time
History was being read from the wrong book.

Vann Scytere

YOU . . . COMPLETE ME
(For Billy)

You're . . . the light that guides me
through all my darkest days,
You're . . . the rail I cling to
whenever I've lost my way,
You're . . . the pillar I lean on
when my strength I cannot find,
You're . . . the arm I hold tightly
when my tear-filled eyes are blind,
You're . . . the beginning of my day
as without out I'd struggle through,
You're . . . the shoulder that carries me
so our future I can view,
You're . . . my branch on the tree of life
that holds me gently close to thee,
You're . . . the grasp that keeps the howling wind
throwing me to nowhere, like other leaves,
You're . . . the one I had dreamt of
long before we met,
You're . . . the one I owe my happiness to
of that, I will never forget,
You're . . . my joy, my hopes, my dreams
I love you beyond compare,
You're . . . my one, my only, my forever
in this deepest love we share,
You're . . . my angel, always at my side
my soulmate, my lover and my best friend
You're . . . my future, my life, 'I love you'
and always will, 'til my life is at an end.

Irene Reid

MY GREAT MUMMY

My mum is always happy
When I get some class points.
I'm sure she was even happy
When she had to change my dirty nappy.

My mum is very helpful
And tries never to be dull.
But she sometimes gets cross
When I don't listen to the boss.

I love sausages very much
My mum cooks them for me.
Even when she is in a rush.
I would eat them for breakfast, lunch and tea.

My mum helps me with everything
Especially with my school homework.
She helps me get through hard times
Like making this poem rhyme.

I love you very much Mummy.
Happy Mother's Day.

Jovan Dulay (7)

MIDNIGHT LOVER

He came to me at midnight
as if upon a steed,
he was eager to devour,
and I, of course, with need.
What passions lie beneath
this skin, pure lust
no love was there,
as sin would have our sorry souls
we didn't even care.
But I, deep in my heart
was seeking love, that's true.
And, in the twilight of my life,
I look around for you.
My midnight lover sought not love
but lust fulfilled his quest.
And, I felt lonelier
once passions spent with zest.
Oh heart, what stories do you weave
with lust mating with love,
and I, of course, felt lonelier
and like a gentle, bleating dove.

Myra Selvadurai

NOISES IN THE NIGHT

When I was young and beautiful, and boys would ask me out,
I didn't know what snoring or sleepwalking was about.
The boys would get themselves all smart, best suits and Elvis hair,
And take me to the pictures, local hops, just everywhere.
We didn't sleep around that time we had more expectations,
And didn't want to shock our mums with unwanted procreations.
So off we set, so very young, to church and take our vows,
Make our promises together that the good book will allow.
But I didn't know that in the night a shocking thing was done,
Funny noises in the bedroom, that wasn't really fun.
As the man that I have married has a habit that is foul,
He's sleep walking in our bedroom, and puts on my face a scowl.
For when his mouth is open, his nostrils really flare,
And I'm sitting up, and looking down, at a snoring grizzly bear.
The years have really changed my man from a model to a chunk,
For he has put lots of weight on, and no longer my young hunk.
The noises that come from his throat are so guttural and profound,
It has taken from our bedroom peace and silence, no more found.
In the quiet of a tomb at night when it's clients are all sleeping,
And insects, rats, and other things are all around us creeping.
My once young, gorgeous husband that was handsome, slim and smart,
Goes to sleep with his mouth open, snores a lot and then he farts.

Wendy Wordsworth (18)

IRELAND'S IMMIGRANT

For countless generations we
have left our homes in search of liberty
forced from our land by hunger, others' greed
persecuted by an alien creed.

We've settled in a far-off place
not always to a friendly face
but in the end no matter where we roam
each country has become an Irish home.

As the years, the centuries have passed
our land now, giving fruit at last
can we look on the misery, of those who flee
come to our shores in pain, their lives to free.

For we among the nations of the world
whose history in blood and death is told
must show compassion, to all those we find
by cruel fate amongst us, though not our kind.

Extend an Irish welcome, from the heart
a helping hand, again their lives to start
as generations of our kin have done
and racism in our land, have none.

B M F

DARK

Dark as the night
with all the noises.
Cloudy as the night
with all the shadows.
Lurid as the night
with all the screams.
Starless as the night
with all the horrors.
Moonless as the night
with all the vastness.
Inky as the night
with all the loneliness.
Murky as the night
praying for daybreak.

Catrina Lawrence

LITTLE ANGEL

A little girl
So innocent
Who never deserved this

A police force
So dedicated
Who needed to catch this

A killer
So cold
Running and hiding from jail

A family
So devastated
By the killer's broken trail

A life
So precious
Taken and torn apart.

Atlanta Oakes

EDITORS

From an amateur killing time, words for fun
To the team read 'News Of The World' in the sun
From thousand poems pick just twenty-five
Perhaps after gone not time while still alive
Are only a number of years, so one gets bored
Waiting so go to the devil or an honoured lord
Truth know little English so few days at school
Own eyes used watching learnt how to use tool
Two years in rectory, found always best honest
Gave life and to a wife did make solemn promise
Richer or poorer, better or worse emptied purse
Left but broke my heart as age becomes curse
You have helped me so much, country's law steal
The country pay police Welsh niece was no deal
My only love for them they learnt to steal show
A lifetime left nothing no boat rough sea no row
Under the waves will no long feel bitter or cold
Thank all for letting me like others grow too old.

John J Flint

JUST BE GLAD

Cry and you cry alone,
Be sad when you're on your own,
So smile, keep your heart light,
Warm the day and keep it bright.
Dance with the wind in your hair,
Show the world how much you care,
Get up and go and be glad,
Life is too precious to be sad.
Always reach for the brightest star in the sky,
Never ask yourself the reason why.
Memories are reflected in our dreams,
Like moonlight dancing in the streams.
Never try to move back,
If you do you'll lose track.
Go forward with your head high,
Never let happiness pass you by.

Margaret Upson

1915

Where has my daddy gone?
I want to see my dad.
Where has Daddy gone? the little boy said.
He left to be a soldier dear
When he left he said, you now have cash for heating
And a little more for bread.

Now we get thirty shillings a week, is that worth fighting for?
We are able to pay the rent man that hammers on the door.

And will he be home at teatime or before I go to bed?
Maybe he will be home for Christmas, that's what my mum said.
Will write and say we love him and he's to hurry back real soon.
Then why are you crying Mum, why are you so sad
Is it what's in that letter Mum,
Is it from my dad?

Gatekeeper

MUSIC OR MENACE

Whatever happened to the sound
of words and beautiful music
that filled the heart with joy and the world with its grace?
Now listen to what has taken its place,
words with no meaning,
it's enough to make you walk upside down on the ceiling.
And a noise that has been put in place of music
each trying so hard to make themselves heard
they drown each other out of place
and for sure do not fill the heart with love and joy,
but make you wish you could hammer away
and smash that music box beyond repair.

Paul Volante

JUST IMAGINE

Just imagine I had wings,
I would fly to meet the king,
Just imagine all the jewels
To steal them, you have to be a fool!
The king would moan,
The queen would groan,
If you can imagine things!

Zahraa Mughal (10)

THE LOVE INSIDE

Take a deep look into my eyes
They reveal a love so true
It's a special love, one of a kind
That's exclusively for you.
It's a certain love like no one knows
And because of you it grows and grows
Growing so big it's hard to hide
Too overwhelming to keep inside
It's a perfect love for us to share
Making us unique, an exceptional pair
It's strength and power are so intense
And without you too, it makes no sense
So please accept this love so true
As this love is a gift from me to you!

Colin Morrow

PHANTOM CROSSWORD SOLVER

I am the phantom crossword solver
The clues yield to my brain's revolver
I slide into the library
And spread *The Times* in front of me
I've been old off, a couple of times
I mustn't desecrate *The Times*
I mustn't spoil the pristine page
But guerrilla warfare I will wage
I keep a pen up my left sleeve
In case I should be asked to leave
I write quick, surreptitiously
I get some sort of childish glee
I did six clues in it today
Then quietly I crept away.

Philip McLynn

APRIL SNOW

Why does it always seem to snow in April
When we thought that springtime was already here,
When we are preparing to sow our summer flowers
Thinking that frosts are something we should no longer fear.

What causes these sudden changes in our climate
When the warm south westerly winds disappear?
And are replaced by icy winds from the north,
And which bring the snow showers that we fear.

It is the jet stream winds which blow high above the Earth
Which determines the way the winds we feel will blow,
An Arctic jet stream will bring the warmth of tropic winds,
But a tropic jet stream will bring northern winds that could mean snow.

If you think that snow in April is unusual,
Then it's time for you to think again,
For the records show it is a regular feature
For snow showers to mingle with the springtime rain.

The spring flowers will be buried in a covering of snow,
But the spring sunshine will quickly make this disappear,
It is all part of nature's weather pattern,
And one that we should expect nearly every year.

R Martin

I SAW YOUR LETTER OF DENIAL
(Dedicated to Faye L Marsden)

Everybody knows you still live in denial
Trying to hide behind your false smile
People say it's so sad and a shame
How you caused us all so much pain.

I knew it when I read that letter
It would get worse instead of better
People tell me about your affair
With the postman - acting so cool - debonair.

He's just another pain killer
To mask your own guilt and pain
Has no idea of your cruel games
You'll pretend to love him the same
Until the pattern repeats itself again.

Then he will also become a victim of your past baggage
He'll end up like a strung out emotional cabbage

Even the postman won't deliver a love like mine
He doesn't know as yet, that you live in denial.

And what you're hiding beneath your tormented smile
It's just a matter of time before *he* ends up on trial.

Graham Hare

SEPARATION

Though we are far apart
And you I cannot see,
The thing that cheers my heart
Is that you think of me.

So if you're overwrought,
Or nothing much to do
Just send a quiet thought
Across to me from you.

And it will cheer my heart
And set my mind at rest
And when reunion comes
You'll find me at my best.

Robert McIlveen

WORRY

Mam doesn't like me climbing trees
She says, I'll scratch my hands and knees.
But I like to climb right to the top
I climb so far then she shouts, 'Stop!'

'Come down, come down you've climbed too high
Are you trying to reach the sky?
Please listen now and come right down
Where you'll be safe back on the ground.

I wish you wouldn't go off on your own
You're far too young to be left alone.
Why don't you play with the kids in the street
And stay on the ground where you're safe on your feet?'

Nicola Joy Moore

LETTER TO THE BETTER

Comfort bides in the
silence of your aloneness.
Your dreams show
poetic possibilities.
Search within the silence,
let your ear find your voice.

Behold your secret self
gazing wide-eyed
and indiscriminate.
Listen and let its wisdom counsel you.
Do this so night's solitude
does not catch you weeping.

Concealed from the natural eye
is your secret self,
relieved of disillusion.
Its light and sturdy spirit
awaits claim to
the empty void within.

Hasten to it
in fear that falsehood
and fabrication
besiege you and attempt
to charm you
with their poisoned tongues.

Nacala Makiin

ANCHOR BOOKS
SUBMISSIONS INVITED
SOMETHING FOR EVERYONE

ANCHOR BOOKS GEN - Any subject,
light-hearted clean fun, nothing unprintable
please.

THE OPPOSITE SEX - Have your say on the
opposite gender. Do they drive you mad or can
we co-exist in harmony?

THE NATURAL WORLD - Are we destroying
the world around us? What should we do to
preserve the beauty and the future of our planet -
you decide!

All poems no longer than 30 lines.
Always welcome! No fee!
Plus cash prizes to be won!

Mark your envelope (eg *The Natural World)*
And send to:
Anchor Books
Remus House, Coltsfoot Drive
Peterborough, PE2 9JX

**OVER £10,000 IN POETRY PRIZES
TO BE WON!**

Send an SAE for details on our latest
competition!